Graduate Education at Historically Black Colleges and Universities (HBCUs)

Highlighting the voices and experiences of Black graduate students at Historically Black Colleges and Universities (HBCUs), this book features the perspectives of students from a variety of academic backgrounds and institutional settings. Contributors discuss their motivation to attend an HBCU for graduate studies, their experiences, and how these helped prepare them for their careers. To be prepared to serve the increasing number of Black students with access to graduate programs at HBCUs, university administrators, faculty, and staff require a better understanding of these students' needs and how to meet them. Addressing some of today's most urgent issues and educational challenges, this book expands the literature on HBCUs and provides insight into the role their graduate schools play in building a diverse academic and professional community.

Robert T. Palmer is associate professor in the Department of Educational Leadership and Policy Studies at Howard University, USA.

Larry J. Walker is an educational consultant focused on supporting historically Black colleges and universities (HBCUs).

Ramon B. Goings is an assistant professor of Educational Leadership at Loyola University, Maryland, USA.

Charmaine Troy is a PhD candidate in higher education at Morgan State University, USA.

Chaz T. Gipson is a PhD student in the School of Communications at Howard University, USA.

Felecia Commodore is assistant professor in Educational Foundations and Leadership at Old Dominion University.

Routledge Research in Higher Education

For a full list of titles in this series, please visit www.routledge.com

16 **Narratives of Doctoral Studies in Science Education**
   Making the transition from educational practitioner to researcher
   Edited by Shirley Simon, Christina Ottander and Ilka Parchmann

17 **Cosmopolitan Learning for a Global Era**
   Higher education in an interconnected world
   Sarah Richardson

18 **Crossing Boundaries and Weaving Intercultural Work, Life, and Scholarship in Globalizing Universities**
   Edited by Adam Komisarof and Zhu Hua

19 **English Studies Beyond the 'Center'**
   Teaching Literature and the Future of Global English
   Myles Chilton

20 **The Working Classes and Higher Education**
   Inequality of Access, Opportunity and Outcome
   Edited by Amy E. Stich and Carrie Freie

21 **Revolutionizing Global Higher Education Policy**
   Innovation and the Bologna Process
   Joseph M. Piro

22 **Working with Underachieving Students in Higher Education**
   Fostering inclusion through narration and reflexivity
   Edited by Maria Francesca Freda, José González Monteagudo and Giovanna Esposito

23 **Graduate Education at Historically Black Colleges and Universities (HBCUs)**
   A Student Perspective
   Edited by Robert T. Palmer, Larry J. Walker, Ramon B. Goings, Charmaine Troy, Chaz T. Gipson, and Felecia Commodore

Graduate Education at Historically Black Colleges and Universities (HBCUs)
A Student Perspective

Edited by
Robert T. Palmer, Larry J. Walker,
Ramon B. Goings, Charmaine Troy,
Chaz T. Gipson, and Felecia Commodore

NEW YORK AND LONDON

First published 2016
by Routledge
711 Third Avenue, New York, NY 10017

and by Routledge
2 Park Square, Milton Park, Abingdon, Oxon, OX14 4RN

First issued in paperback 2018

Routledge is an imprint of the Taylor & Francis Group, an informa business

© 2016 Taylor & Francis

The right of Robert T. Palmer, Larry J. Walker, Ramon B. Goings, Charmaine Troy, Chaz T. Gipson, and Felecia Commodore to be identified as editors of this work has been asserted by them in accordance with sections 77 and 78 of the Copyright, Designs and Patents Act 1988.

All rights reserved. No part of this book may be reprinted or reproduced or utilised in any form or by any electronic, mechanical, or other means, now known or hereafter invented, including photocopying and recording, or in any information storage or retrieval system, without permission in writing from the publishers.

Trademark notice: Product or corporate names may be trademarks or registered trademarks, and are used only for identification and explanation without intent to infringe.

Library of Congress Cataloging-in-Publication Data
Names: Palmer, Robert T., editor.
Title: Graduate education at historically black colleges and
　　universities (HBCUs) : a student perspective / edited by Robert T.
　　Palmer, Larry J. Walker, Ramon B. Goings, Charmaine Troy, Chaz
　　T. Gipson and Felecia Commodore.
Description: New York, NY : Routledge, 2016. | Series: Routledge
　　research in higher education ; 23
Identifiers: LCCN 2016000868 | ISBN 9781138959606 (hbk) |
　　ISBN 9781315648859 (ebk)
Subjects: LCSH: African Americans—Education (Graduate) | African
　　American graduate students. | African American universities and
　　colleges—Graduate work. | Universities and colleges—
　　United States—Graduate work.
Classification: LCC LC2781 .G68 2016 |
　　DDC 378.1/982996073—dc23
LC record available at http://lccn.loc.gov/2016000868

ISBN 13: 978-1-138-60022-5 (pbk)
ISBN 13: 978-1-138-95960-6 (hbk)

Typeset in Sabon
by Apex CoVantage, LLC

Contents

Foreword vii
TERENCE HICKS

Acknowledgments ix

Introduction xi

1 Contextualizing Graduate Education at Historically Black Colleges and Universities 1
ROBERT T. PALMER, LARRY J. WALKER, RAMON B. GOINGS, CHARMAINE TROY, CHAZ T. GIPSON, AND FELECIA COMMODORE

2 A Strange Song in a Familiar Land 15
LAMAR HYLTON

3 Journey to the PhD: A Personal Narrative of Doctoral Studies at an HBCU 25
TIFFANY F. BOYKIN

4 Graduate-Level Education at Historically Black Colleges and Universities: A Three-Part Qualitative Exposition 39
ANTONIO L. ELLIS, CHRISTOPHER N. SMITH, AND JANATUS A. BARNETT

5 Back to the Roots 55
SHEREE ALEXANDER

6 Praise for the Bridge: My Doctoral Journey at Morgan State University 70
KIMBERLY HARDY

7 Free to Conduct Research of Race and Racism in My West Baltimore Community 79
JULIUS DAVIS

8 The Historically Black College and University Family: A Perspective on a Graduate-Level Online Accelerated Cohort Program   90
KIMBERLY R. ELDRIDGE

9 Twice the Experiences: Graduate School at Two Comprehensive HBCUs   102
STEVIE L. LAWRENCE II

10 The Significant Value of Historically Black Colleges and Universities   113
TARA D. MILLER

11 A Liberating Spirituality: Evaluating Theological Education at a Black Graduate School   124
HERBERT ROBINSON MARBURY

12 Strange Fruit: The Contribution of the Historically Black College and University (HBCU) to the Development of the Black Intelligentsia   133
F. ABRON FRANKLIN

About the Editors   141
About the Contributors   145
Index   149

Foreword

Terence Hicks

The overall mission of Historically Black College and Universities (HBCUs) plays a vital role in providing educational opportunities for Blacks who would otherwise be denied access to college (Redd, 2000). Until the midpoint of the twentieth century, more than 90 percent of the Black students enrolled in higher education in this country were educated in HBCUs (National Center for Education Statistics, 1996).

HBCUs are essential in providing a supportive and nurturing environment for Black students, regardless of their academic and social circumstances. Furthermore, HBCUs have been known to provide the kind of academic and social environment that many Blacks need to survive and persist through college. As a current dean of a College of Education at a predominantly White institution (PWI) and as a former dean of a College of Education at an Historically Black University, I am aware of the role that both PWIs and HBCUs play in providing quality graduate programs to its students. There are extraordinary Black students in graduate programs across this nation who are academically outstanding and will be sure to make a difference in their careers and communities. Whereas previous research has contributed to our understanding of the impact that HBCUs have on Black undergraduate students, the literature is limited when it comes to highlighting the voices and experiences of Black graduate students. Palmer, Walker, Goings, Troy, Gipson, and Commodore edited this volume, entitled *Graduate Education at Historically Black Colleges and Universities (HBCUs): A Student Perspective*, which helps fills that void by introducing the perspectives of graduate students from a variety of academic backgrounds and institutional settings. As colleges and universities are welcoming more and more students within their graduate programs, the number of Black students who have access to these programs will continue to increase. With this in mind, university administrators, faculty, and staff must be prepared to serve these students. Through current research, these university officials can achieve a better understanding of what Black students at the graduate level need. Thus, it would be helpful to know what educational challenges exist for these students upon entering graduate school.

The Palmer et al. edited volume is an excellent start to gain an understanding. Their book provides a better understanding of graduate education at HBCUs through voices of individuals who are currently enrolled in graduate programs at HBCUs or who have pursed graduate studies at an HBCU. Furthermore, Palmer et al. called upon a wide range of contributors to provide narratives that highlighted their motivation to attend an HBCU for their graduate education and revealed how their institutions prepared them for current and future career success. Anyone interested in the state of graduate education in HBCUs and its effects on Black students should have a vested interest in this volume. The editors addresses some of today's most urgent issues facing Black graduate students at HBCUs, and this book will not only expand the literature on graduate education at HBCUs but will also serve as an important text for a variety of higher education courses. As an academic dean, I highly recommend that this volume to be included in university and college bookstores across the United States and placed on the bookshelves of all Black graduate students as they matriculate through their respective programs.

Terence Hicks, PhD, EdD
Dean, Claudius G. Clemmer College of Education
East Tennessee State University

References

National Center for Education Statistics. (1996). *Historically Black colleges and universities, 1976–1994*. Washington, DC: U.S. Department of Education.

Redd, K. E. (2000). *HBCU graduates: Employment, earnings, and success after college*. Indianapolis, IN: USA Group Foundation.

Acknowledgments

Robert T. Palmer: I want to acknowledge the authors for sharing their stories in this book and thank my coeditors for their hard work. This book is dedicated to Omar Manneh for showing me how to smile again. I love you!

Larry J. Walker: This book is dedicated to my wife, Nicola, and son, Jacob, for all their patience and support. They keep me grounded and motivated. Family plays an integral role in my life, and sharing each accomplishment pushes me harder to succeed. Collectively they are the bedrock I stand upon. I look forward to continuing our journey together. I would like to acknowledge my fellow coeditors, Dr. Robert T. Palmer, Dr. Ramon B. Goings, Ms. Charmaine Troy, Mr. Chaz Gipson, and Dr. Felecia Commodore for their commitment to HBCUs. In addition, special thanks to the administrators, faculty, and staff at Cheyney University, Howard University, and Morgan State University for encouraging me to challenge economic, political, and social constructs. Despite the obstacles, HBCUs continue to produce change agents committed to deconstructing national and international issues.

Ramon B. Goings: This book is dedicated to my lovely wife, Renee. Your support and encouragement keep me grounded and motivated to make an impact on the world. Last, this book is dedicated to the late brother Adedire Asosanya, a bright young Morgan State student, fraternity brother, and personal friend who lost his life too soon. First I would like to thank my fellow coeditors, Dr. Robert Palmer, Dr. Larry Walker, Mr. Chaz Gipson, Ms. Charmaine Troy, and Dr. Felicia Commodore, for their hard work and dedication to the development of this book. I would also like to give special thanks to my professors in the Department of Advanced Studies, Leadership, and Policy at Morgan State University for nurturing and supporting my development as an emerging scholar. The sacrifices you all made for my scholarly development continue to build on the legacy of HBCUs and their ability to develop Black scholars prepared to tackle pressing issues impacting the Black community.

Charmaine Troy: This work is dedicated to my daughter, Dominique Bell, without whose love and support it would not have been possible, and my mother, Henrietta Troy, who instilled in me strength, knowledge, and a love for education.

Chaz T. Gipson: This book is dedicated to prospective HBCU graduate students who will seek the light to advance their education. I also acknowledge the graduate faculty from Howard University's School of Education and School of Communications for challenging my intellectual mind-set and preparing me for excellence within and outside of the academic walls.

Felicia Commodore: Anytime I am given the opportunity to aid in creating a platform for HBCU voices to be heard, it is a privilege. I would like to thank Rob Palmer for the opportunity to work alongside him and all the brilliant scholars who made this book come to fruition. You have been a great colleague and mentor, and I am ever grateful for every chance I get to work with you. I would also like to thank my other fellow coeditors, Ramon, Chaz, Larry, and Charmaine. What great company in which to be included, and I look forward to collaborating for years to come. I would also like to thank all the authors who contributed. Your hard work and dedication are appreciated. And thank you to my friends who push me, my family who prays for me, and my roommate, Nekeya, who puts up with me. I dedicate this book to anyone who has heard no far more times than yes. Sometimes it takes hearing no to push you to where you are supposed to be, and it only takes one yes to launch you into your destiny.

Introduction

The purpose of the book is to provide meaningful context on graduate education at historically Black colleges and universities (HBCUs). In order to achieve this objective, my colleagues and I encouraged chapter contributors to discuss their experiences as graduate students at HBCUs. Specifically, chapter contributors focused on reasons they attended HBCUs for graduate education, their experiences and challenges at these institutions, the extent that HBCUs prepared them for postgraduate life, and the importance of discussing and examining graduate education at HBCUs. The book consists of twelve chapters. In chapter 1, Robert T. Palmer, Larry J. Walker, Ramon Goings, Charmaine Troy, Chaz Gipson, and Felecia Commodore not only discuss the significance and overall intent of this book, but they also give insight into their experiences as graduate students at HBCUs. This chapter concludes by discussing implications for future research on graduate education at HBCUs.

In chapter 2, Lamar Hylton focuses on the journey of a doctoral student attending the same institution in which he received his undergraduate degree. Specifically, he explores issues of navigating the cultural and political landscape of a familiar institution, the tension felt during personal and professional transitions, and the lessons he learned that assisted in his career trajectory. In chapter 3, Tiffany F. Boykin presents a narrative of her journey to the PhD at an HBCU. She delineates the impact that faculty interaction had on cultivating a positive academic and social experience at her HBCU. Her chapter concludes with recommendations for prospective HBCU doctoral students.

In chapter 4, Antonio L. Ellis, Christopher N. Smith, and Janatus A. Barnett reflect on their experiences as graduate students at HBCUs. One of the most compelling narratives of this chapter is Ellis's story of being encouraged by professors not to attend an HBCU for graduate school. Ellis notes that his professors suggested that people who receive graduate degrees from HBCUs are less likely to be employed compared to persons who studied at predominantly White institutions (PWIs). Unfortunately, Ellis took the advice of these professors seriously. Therefore, after completing his undergraduate work at an HBCU, he attended a PWI for his graduate degree but transferred back to an HBCU due to experiences with incivility from faculty and administrators. In essence, this chapter is a testament to the important role of graduate education at HBCUs.

In chapter 5, Sheree Alexander focuses on her journey to school leadership beginning with her experiences attending a PWI and later, an HBCU for graduate school. Her chapter is a testament to the important role that HBCUs play in cultivating an affirming, caring, and nurturing environment for graduate students. Her chapter also speaks to how HBCUs prepare students to be leaders within the urban community. In chapter 6, Kimberly Hardy delineates how the faculty and staff at the HBCU she attended for graduate school would not allow her to choose mediocrity. She also reflects on the transformation that occurred when she realized that faculty at her HBCU were truly invested in her success.

In chapter 7, Julius Davis discusses how his desire to revitalize his community led him to an HBCU for his doctoral education. The chapter also highlights how faculty members provided an intellectual environment where he received support to conduct research on the intersection between Black students' mathematical experiences, race, and racism. Last, his chapter underscores how attending an HBCU provides an opportunity to conduct liberatory research that not only impacts Black students in schools but also the communities where they reside. In chapter 8, Kimberly R. Eldridge explores the perspective of a doctoral student at an HBCU in the southeastern United States. Specifically, her chapter discusses the role of the cohort model, the role of an online program, and how this online/cohort model might affect the success of the student. Her chapter also gives attention to the role and value of the HBCU family, the overall learning process, and the importance of the online/cohort model of the graduate program.

In chapter 9, Stevie L. Lawrence II highlights the uniqueness of the graduate school experience at both of the HBCUs he attended. His chapter focuses on the success of both graduate programs nationally, detailed personal accounts, and how pursuing graduate education at these institutions has contributed to his personal, spiritual, and professional development. In conjunction with these points, his chapter highlights the motivation for attending graduate school at an HBCU, along with providing recommendations for students considering attending graduate school at an historically Black institution. In chapter 10, Tara D. Miller discusses her experience as a graduate student at two HBCUs. Important themes in her chapter include how HBCUs are incubators for developing brilliant scholastic minds. She also focuses on how critics try to disparage the rich reputations of administrators, faculty, and students at these important institutions. Critical to her chapter is the role that faculty play in the development of students' educational pathways to success.

In chapter 11, Herbert Robinson Marbury offers a critical perspective on his experience as a student at Interdenominational Theological Center (ITC), which has been the largest predominantly Black professional graduate

Introduction xiii

school of theology. Specifically, his chapter focuses on aspects of the school's mission that compelled him to enroll. Moreover, he also discusses his experience at ITC as a student. Finally, he reflects on how the school prepared him for his current vocational life. In the last chapter, F. Abron Franklin articulates the role of the HBCU in the development of the Black intelligentsia. He particular, he emphasizes that HBCUs create a safe space for advancing the intellectual imagination and intellectual resiliency of the Black graduate student.

1 Contextualizing Graduate Education at Historically Black Colleges and Universities

Robert T. Palmer, Larry J. Walker, Ramon B. Goings, Charmaine Troy, Chaz T. Gipson, and Felecia Commodore

In 2012, my colleagues and I released a book on graduate education at Historically Black Colleges and Universities (HBCUs). We thought this book was critical because little research had provided context on graduate education at HBCUs. Having attended an HBCU for our doctoral degrees, we wish we had a book that provided a holistic view of graduate education at HBCUs when we thought about attending one for our graduate education. Whereas we felt that this book, *Black Graduate Education at Historically Black Colleges and Universities: Trends, Experiences, and Outcomes*, was critical and offered necessary insight into HBCU graduate education, we thought we had inadvertently limited the accessibility of this book because it was weighted down by academic jargon. This limitation birthed the idea for this current book, *Graduate Education at Historically Black Colleges and Universities: A Student Perspective*.

Whereas both books are immensely important to the scholarly discourse on HBCUs, this book is different because students who attended HBCUs for their graduate education are providing a personal scholarly narrative to offer insight into their experiences of pursuing graduate education at HBCUs. This book, as well as the latter, is integral because it helps to demystify graduate education at HBCUs. In recent years, there has been a proliferation of academic and nonacademic publications on HBCUs. These sources have explored a wealth of topics, including the overall relevance of HBCUs to the landscape of higher education, leadership and faculty governance, and the experiences of diverse student populations.

A frequent theme in some of HBCU literature, which is often cited to highlight the value-added aspect of HBCUs, is their ability to admit students who are academically underprepared and graduate them with the skills to enter the most competitive predominantly White institutions (PWIs) for graduate school (*The Educational Effectiveness of Historically Black colleges and Universities*, 2010). Whereas discussing the value-added component of HBCUs is critical, this characterization seems to imply that graduate education at HBCUs is somehow inferior to their PWI counterparts. Moreover, there have been articles published in prominent new publications (e.g.,

Wall Street Journal) that have attacked HBCUs for their low graduation rates, mismanagement of funding, and being irrelevant in today's higher education landscape without acknowledging how these institutions graduate thousands of Black students each year while being inequitably funded by state and federal government. Although not specifically targeting HBCU graduate education, these articles have the propensity to hinder the number of students enrolling in HBCUs to pursue graduate studies.

The purpose of this book as well as this chapter is to provide some authentic context about graduate education at HBCUs. To do this, the subsequent part of this chapter will review the limited literature on HBCU graduate education. Five personal narratives of chapter authors who pursued graduate education at HBCUs will follow this review of literature. These narratives will provide insight into reasons the authors attended graduate education at HBCUs and discuss their experiences. This chapter will conclude with thoughts about graduate education at HBCUs and discuss future research possibilities.

Brief Review of the Literature on HBCU Graduate Education

Admittedly, empirical research on graduate education is quite limited (Gasman & Williams, 2012; Lundy-Wagner, 2012). Nevertheless, a few scholarly articles have focused on HBCU graduate education. For example, Fountaine (2008) used a seven-part questionnaire to examine factors related to persistence and the academic experiences of 190 doctoral students across thirteen public and private HBCUs. Some of the factors included in the questionnaire were the student's background, pre-enrollment, financing, student-faculty interaction, student-peer interaction, doctoral experience, and time to degree completion. Her findings revealed the importance of managing the expectations of students before enrollment, the significance of meaningful faculty-student interactions, and how positive interactions with peers were critical to the success of doctoral students at HBCUs. Similarly, in a qualitative study that investigated the enrollment decisions and educational experiences of eight students who pursued graduate education at HBCUs (seven of whom earned their doctoral degrees from HBCUs), Palmer (2012) found that faculty-student interaction and positive encounters with peers were vital factors to the success of the participants in his study. Despite this, however, participants complained about the lack of customer service from staff, condescending interactions with administrators, and lack of resource parity with their PWI counterparts. In spite of this, they highly valued their HBCU graduate experience. Some even received all or most of all their degrees from HBCUs.

In addition to research highlighting the importance of meaningful faculty-student interaction and positive peer support on the success of graduate students at HBCUs, research has shown that 9 percent of full-time Black faculty earned their doctorate degrees from HBCUs and that more than half return to HBCUs as faculty members (Perna, 2001). This finding is noteworthy and highlights the critical role that graduate education at HBCUs plays in producing Black faculty. The student body of graduate programs at HBCUs is quite diverse. First, it is important to note that graduate programs at HBCUs have historically enrolled a large number of individuals who are non-Black (Provasnik, Shafer, & Snyder, 2004). Indeed, according to Conrad, Brier, and Braxton (1997), more than 20 percent of HBCU graduate students were White in 2002. The student diversity of HBCU graduate programs might be somewhat higher today given that the student populations of HBCUs in general have become more diverse (Gasman et al., 2013; Palmer & Maramba, 2015a, 2015b).

Whereas research has shown that HBCUs provide supportive environments for graduate students (e.g., Fountaine, 2008) as discussed, very little is known about the experiences of graduate students attending HBCUs. Moreover, there are limited scholarly contributions that explore the HBCU experience from firsthand accounts of individuals who have attended them. Starting with our own experiences attending HBCUs for graduate school, we believe this book will provide the reader with detailed information about how to navigate the HBCU campus environment and how these institutions have prepared and propelled us for future success.

Personal Scholarly Narratives

Robert T. Palmer

I initially became interested in attending an HBCU for my undergraduate experience because I was interested in learning more about my culture as a Black man. In high school, teachers talked slavery and the civil rights movement, but aside from this, they did not provide a comprehensive lesson on the achievements and many contributions Blacks made to the United States. Thus, by attending an HBCU, I was seeking cultural empowerment. To this end, I made sure to include an HBCU among the colleges I applied to for my baccalaureate degree. Whereas I was admitted into that HBCU, my mother thought I should attend a PWI because she felt that the quality of education would be better. Being young and naïve, I did not challenge her thinking; I acquiesced.

After I completed my baccalaureate degree, I attended graduate school for my master's degree at another PWI. It was there I started to research HBCUs more intensively. My research of HBCUs revealed that they provided an empowering environment that helped to facilitate a sense of role modeling, leadership development, cultural nourishment, psychological wellness, and academic success for Black students in general and Black men in particular. These aspects intrigued me greatly and made me yearn even more for a "taste" of the HBCU experience. This was especially true because most of my experiences at PWIs were void of some of these characteristics. Whereas I was successful academically at the PWIs I attended, most of my experiences were marred by racial microaggressions and alienation, which resulted in psychological fatigue.

Given that the PhD represented one of my last opportunities to get a sense of the HBCU experience, I decided to pursue a doctoral degree at an HBCU. Before attending, however, I had some major misconceptions about graduate education at an HBCU. One of the main misconceptions stemmed from funding or lack thereof. Because most of the literature emphasized that HBCUs, particularly public HBCUs, were underfunded compared to the PWI counterparts, I thought I would have to take out a loan to fund my doctoral degree. This was far from the truth. When I was admitted into my program at the HBCU I attended, I received a graduate assistantship, which paid me a small stipend and with the exception of fees, covered my tuition.

When I started my PhD program, I was amazed at how different my experiences were from the experiences at the PWIs I had attended. For one, many of the faculty members in my program were Black or Latino. This was totally different from my educational experience, especially at the two PWIs I had attended. Having faculty with whom I was able to identify motivated me because it let me know that I could actually earn my PhD because they had done so too. Is this regard, these faculty members became my source of inspiration, encouragement, and resiliency. They were also tougher on me than faculty at the PWIs I had attended. When I doubted myself, they pushed me to excel and helped me to discover untapped potential. Aside from this, the faculty in my program also created a family-oriented environment. This sense of family support manifested itself in different ways. For example, one year, a professor in my program knew I was going to be alone for the Thanksgiving holiday. As a result, he ordered food for one of my classes just before the semester break. The class was rather small, but he ordered a large amount of food. After we ate as a class, he asked me to take the leftovers home because he wanted me to have a Thanksgiving meal over the holiday break. I was so appreciative of his thoughtfulness and fatherly interactions. The family support I experienced from the faculty in my PhD program played an integral role in my success, and it is one of the reasons I am so passionate about researching and advocating for HBCUs today.

Aside from faculty support, the friendships that I made with peers in my PhD program were another defining aspect of my experience in my graduate program at the HBCU. These relationships were different than the ones I had formed with peers at the PWI I had attended for my master's. In that program, there were only a few Black students, and I would often be the only Black person in my class. Being the only one was particularly problematic when we had to do group work; in this situation I would often be the last person my peers would select for assignments. Moreover, when I was a part of a group, being the only Black person, I felt that I had to work harder than my peers to disprove the stereotypical notion that Blacks were lazy and intellectually inept.

The relationships, however, I formed with peers in my PhD program were void of these issues. The aspect that excited me most was the fact that we were young, ambitious, Black and Brown students, striving to earn "the three magic letters": PhD. These commonalities resulted in us forming supportive and nurturing bonds, which helped me to get through some difficult times in my program and played a salient role in my ability to earn my PhD in higher education administration in 2007.

Larry J. Walker

HBCUs played a vital role preparing me for a variety of societal challenges. For instance, my experience as a graduate student at Howard University taught me how swift demographic changes can alter the social fabric of established neighborhoods, whereas my tenure at Morgan State University highlighted the importance of closing racial gaps. My time at Howard provided the opportunity to work with the local community to examine how changes in the racial composition of the city will impact underserved communities. The enriching experiences at both institutions were consistent with my undergraduate experience attending the nation's oldest HBCU, Cheyney University. Although some pundits lament the importance of HBCUs in today's society, I benefited from attending HBCUs located in urban enclaves with a focus on social justice. Thus, I learned to deconstruct economic, educational, political, and social issues that continue to hamper efforts to improve conditions in neighborhoods. In retrospect, I'm glad I didn't allow my apprehension of attending two HBCUs for graduate school to influence my decision after completing my bachelor's degree. Based on conversations with colleagues who attended PWIs, I realize the nurturing HBCU environment helped propel my career.

There are a few distinct experiences related to attending HBCUs for graduate school that helped to shape my professional experiences. During my tenure at Howard, a fellow student brought to my attention a fellowship opportunity that changed my life. Eventually I applied and was selected for a congressional fellowship with the Congressional Black Caucus Foundation. This life-changing experience allowed me to interact with powerful national and international leaders. After several years of working in politics, I applied the skills from my policy experience to improving conditions in communities of color. Attending Howard was directly related to my time working on Capitol Hill. Professors and colleagues encouraged me to apply to the program and lay the foundation for the next generation of change agents.

Encouraging me to seek out the fellowship opportunity is consistent with strong support system at HBCUs. They provide critical academic and emotional scaffolding that sustains students through long, cold winters and hot summers that frequently prevent Black students from completing their graduate education. Howard and Morgan gave me an opportunity to excel in encouraging, competitive environments designed to bring out the best in every student. Committed students worked together inside and outside the classroom to solve issues that negatively impact the Black community.

There are a number of occasions when I have spent tireless hours collaborating with classmates on school- and community-related projects. For example, while at Howard I helped to design and implement a literacy-based summer program to improve the skills of students in Washington, DC. In addition, Morgan State supported efforts to examine the factors that contributed to the events following the death of Freddie Gray in Baltimore. The strong emphasis on social justice is consistent with HBCUs mission to support the surrounding community.

The focus on communalism and mentorship drew me to both institutions for graduate school. Professors and students from both schools were committed to working evening and weekends to encourage students struggling with academic or personal issues. I learned that once you were part of the academic community, individuals would sacrifice time and effort to ensure you were successful. My relationship with professors was the key to my success. Developing strong bonds with scholars of color is an invaluable experience in today's society. Professors encouraged me to work harder without making assumptions about my ability to complete my graduate degree.

I am forever indebted to the administrators, faculty, and staff members who found the time to invest in my future. Without their consistent positive feedback, I may have failed to obtain my master's and doctorate. For this reason, it is vital that HBCUs receive federal, state and local support to increase the number of college graduates from low- and moderate-income families. HBCUs have a track record of enrolling and graduating students with minimal family and community support. They hold the key to increasing the number of students with graduate degrees in critical need areas. This book provides a platform for successful HBCU graduates to share their triumphs and struggles with a new generation of students. It is an important project that will provide faculty members and researchers with a guide to help new and returning graduate students.

Ramon Goings

After obtaining my master's degree, entering a doctoral program was the last thing on my mind. However, during a conversation with a family member (Dr. Payne), she began discussing her experiences in her doctoral program at an HBCU and thought I should consider continuing my education. After much thought, I began to research programs. Initially I was unsure of the degree I wanted to pursue; however, because I was serving as a special education teacher in an urban school district, I thought completing a program in urban education would allow me to better serve my students. Through my research, there were several programs that appealed to me, but it was Morgan State University's (MSU) focus on addressing issues impacting urban schools that stuck out to me most.

As a result of attending two PWIs for my bachelor's and master's degrees, I was in desperate need of an education that embraced the contributions of Blacks in education. For far too long I was immersed in an education that solely embraced a Eurocentric viewpoint. I didn't have the opportunity to read any literature by Black Americans in any of my courses. More importantly, I never felt fully invested in these subjects because my cultural experiences were not reflected in my reading materials; thus I felt that my experience did not matter in those fields. Attending MSU provided an opportunity for me to find my Black consciousness.

My Student Experience at MSU

MSU was a perfect fit for me because my classes were focused on the ways in which Black Americans have contributed to the education field. I needed the exposure to reeducate myself. In addition, this was the opportunity to be taught by Black professors generally, and males specifically. This was my first opportunity to envision myself as a college professor.

As a student, I had the opportunity to interact with professors with similar interests. For instance, during a presentation in qualitative research, my professor brought in a guest lecturer to discuss his research and qualitative methods. Because this scholar focused on issues around Black males, I believed he would be the perfect mentor to support my scholarly development. After our first encounter, this professor and I developed a rapport and presented at international and national conferences and have written several journal articles together. I am not sure that if I attended a non-HBCU I would have had the opportunity to make this type of connection. My MSU professor believed that in order to become scholars, we had to be surrounded by scholars from MSU and outside of the institution. It was these types of mentorship opportunities that propelled me to persist in my doctoral program. I knew I was not only continuing my program for me but to show my mentors that their investment would not be in vain.

Preparing for the Future

During my final year in the doctoral program when I was completing my dissertation research on the academic and social experiences of high-achieving Black males attending HBCUs, my peers and faculty were always there to support me. For instance, one of my classmates and fellow coeditor of this book (Dr. Walker) and I always worked together and pushed each other to get through the dissertation phase. Because we started the program together, we developed our own cohort to ensure we did not leave the other behind. Not only did our relationship result in me completing my dissertation, but we have also continued to support each other as we explore various research and employment opportunities.

HBCUs, for many reasons described in the opening of this chapter, have been under attack. However, this book provides the reader with a direct counter-narrative that shows how HBCUs prepare students for success in their chosen careers. I know that without attending an HBCU, I may have never thought to conduct research on Black males at these institutions. Because of my positive experiences at MSU, I will always serve as an advocate for HBCUs.

Charmaine Troy

Making the decision to enroll into a doctoral program was a choice accompanied by a mixture of excitement, doubt, and preparation for change. The process was met with both challenges and positive experiences. Selecting an institution that met my needs and the ability to finance the degree added to the challenge of seeking the doctorate degree. After receiving my bachelor's degree from a PWI and my master's degree from an HBCU, I had to make the decision on which type of institution to attend. There were many perks to attending a PWI as an undergraduate student that I enjoyed. For example, I enjoyed the minority programs on campus and the camaraderie among minority students. There was an overwhelming amount of resources that the school offered for its students. There were also ample resources for financing my undergraduate degree. However, many of the experiences I enjoyed during my undergraduate years were outside of the classroom. There was a shortage of minority professors in the classroom, leaving me with no opportunity to learn from someone who looked like me. In addition to that, there were limited opportunities to receive guidance from professors during and after class due to class size.

In comparison to my experience at a PWI during my undergraduate years was my experience as a master's student at an HBCU. My journey of change began with opting to try attending an HBCU for my master's degree after ten years of working. I heard about the experience of attending an HBCU from some friends who chose to attend them during our undergraduate years. However, I wanted to experience the journey for myself. My journey was one of inclusion and satisfaction inside and outside of the classroom. I felt welcomed by faculty and staff. I felt of a sense of inclusion from faculty during class and much-needed guidance outside of the classroom. All of these positive experiences during my master's program played a part in my decision to enroll in an HBCU for my doctorate degree. However, the challenges of financing the degree and limited graduate assistantships almost dissuaded me from applying to Morgan State University. Ultimately, my decision to attend Morgan State as a doctoral student was due to the ability to receive graduate funding, the availability of my program of choice, and cost.

The Journey of Change and Acceptance

I began the doctoral program at Morgan State during the summer. I recall my first day of class and how nervous I was. It was probably not in my best interest to begin the doctoral program in the summer due to limited courses and no workshops for new students. However, I made the best of it by talking to my classmates about their experiences in the program on my first day. Consequently, I began to navigate the doctoral program the way that I knew how: networking with students, faculty, and administrators on campus; reading the required material; completing coursework; and being active in class discussion. Little did I know that in order to be successful on the journey, I would be required to go beyond my level of comfort. My journey required a change in not only lifestyle but also acceptance of what it meant to obtain a PhD. It also meant connecting with other scholars outside of Morgan State University in order to gain writing opportunities.

Eliminating Self-Doubt

As a master's student, I was very confident in my ability to navigate the program. Scholars have suggested that that it takes the entire institutional village to produce competent, successful graduates (Hale, 2006). I attribute my success to the positive interactions I had with my graduate faculty at North Carolina Central University. As a result of my positive interactions with my graduate faculty, I experienced success in my course work and related endeavors. However, I arrived to the doctoral program full of self-doubt about my ability to complete the journey. Specifically, I questioned myself on my ability to keep up with coursework, complete the dissertation, and raise my child all at the same time. I was able to overcome my self-doubt through universal inclusion, thought-provoking conversations, nurturing relationships with faculty and administrators, and defining my research agenda with faculty.

My decision to attend an HBCU is one of the best decisions that I have ever made. Enrolling into an HBCU for graduate education had its ups and downs but has been a rewarding experience overall.

Chaz T. Gipson

I attended an HBCU because it was introduced to me as the experience of a lifetime and a way of escape, personal growth, and professional development. While growing up, I faced many challenges that first-generation lower-income students face. I grew up in public housing and was often bullied by the "cool kids" in school. Growing up in a single-parent household, I did not reap the benefits typically afforded to those who constantly have the wisdom and simple assurances provided by a father figure or any other male role model, which sometimes made my journey into manhood challenging. In addition, I often watched my mother struggle to make ends meet so we could survive. Other than my teachers and other school professionals, I did not cross paths with people with college backgrounds, credentials, or professional degrees, which occasionally caused me to question my ability to succeed. In high school, my counselor introduced me to the TRIO program, which eventually afforded me the opportunity to attend college. TRIO programs are federal outreach and student service programs designed to identify and provide services for students from disadvantaged backgrounds.

Attending an HBCU for my undergraduate studies and participating in TRIO-Talent Search, Upward Bound, and Student Support Services were all very essential to my growth and development as a scholar; however, my acceptance into the Ronald E. McNair Post-Baccalaureate Scholarship Program became a major turning point in my life in terms of my pursuit of a doctoral degree. The Ronald E. McNair Scholarship Program seeks to increase the attainment of post-baccalaureate degrees from underrepresented segments of society. During my time in the program, in addition to academic counseling and activities designed to assist scholars in securing admissions and financial assistance, I was introduced to graduate study and other opportunities during an intensive summer research experience. This experience, along with great mentorship, resulted in my participation in the Fifteenth Annual Southeastern Association of Educational Opportunity Program (SAEOPP) Research Conference. There, I presented on my research topic "How Do Health Beliefs Affect Health Behaviors among African American Male College Students." I left the convening as the first-place winner for the Division of Social & Behavioral Sciences and received the Ronald E. McNair Award of Excellence. Mrs. Cheryl McNair, the wife of Ronald McNair, told me how proud she was to see another Black male doing great things and that I was destined for that PhD.

Afterward, I enrolled into an HBCU on the East Coast. When I was first accepted into graduate school, I was dubious. I applied with skepticism, partly because I wanted "diversity." I made the mistake of believing the diversity of a college or university was only found in the students' variety of skin color and race. Coming from a predominantly Black neighborhood and a diverse city and completing my undergraduate education at an HBCU, I thought I had experienced a multitude of perspectives in regard to the various topics I have conducted research on over the years. However, as I attended my HBCU graduate orientation, I was astonished by the beauty, intelligence, and compassion of my future graduate colleagues who were hungry for success. Being on campus and seeing so many scholarly graduate students of color with advanced research profiles and interests deepened my desire to be around my own people in this inspiring and collegial environment. When I actually began my graduate studies, I felt challenged, intellectually and politically, and it happened not at Brown, not at Harvard, and not at Georgetown, but at another HBCU. Additionally, I knew that I wanted to dedicate my life to helping students who looked just like me. Driven by the belief that my true talent was rooted somewhere within the realm of academia, and my contribution to my generation and society would be formulated and strengthened within the walls of classrooms surrounded by peers who challenged me on an even more advanced level, I quickly emerged into the graduate culture at my HBCU with much more motivation, determination, and care.

Once I was admitted into the graduate program at the HBCU that I decided to attend, I received a graduate assistantship working partially in graduate admissions and partially in student life and affairs. This covered my tuition and paid a $20,000 stipend. Additionally, I worked in Residence Life as a graduate resident's advisor, which covered my housing and meal plan. As I successfully matriculated throughout graduate school, I completed my master's in education and was offered an opportunity to enroll into the PhD program, fully funded, in exchange for teaching a few undergraduate courses. Already having an established community with a budding circle of friends and aspiring scholars, along with consistent mentorship from faculty members who truly cared about my success, I wholeheartedly embraced my doctoral studies.

Through perseverance, resilience, and determination I have reached the midpoint in my doctoral studies, while working full time to take care of my mother, Regina Gipson, who suffered with lupus. Sadly, she transitioned on January 1, 2015. When she passed, I was distraught and no longer had a desire to continue my doctoral studies. Faculty members, mentors, and friends in the HBCU graduate community were very encouraging, understanding, and supportive during this time. These past few months have been beyond rough, and I struggle daily, wondering in sorrow how I will continue to make it. I constantly replay in my mind her last few words to me: "Chaz, promise me that you will get your doctorate degree and make a major difference in the field of higher education and the world as you have always dreamed." As I struggle to write this statement, it is written in her honor. After taking nearly a year away from my HBCU graduate education, I have resumed with full force, yet I remember the last words of my mother and the commitment I made as a Ronald McNair Scholar, which is to pursue and obtain my PhD. Additionally, I have been named as a current White House HBCU ALL-STAR, which is an initiative started by the Obama administration to highlight HBCU student trailblazers.

If it had not been for TRIO, all of my supportive mentors, my close relatives, the HBCU community experience, and my mother, I do not think I would be as far along in reaching the goals I have set. I will continue to serve God, work hard, give back to my community by being a role model for others, advocate for HBCUs while encouraging my undergraduate students and mentees to consider attending an HBCU for their graduate education, and strive for excellence in all I attempt to do. Last, I will ensure that my mother, Regina Gipson's last wishes are realized and make my success happen as a tribute to her, knowing she is smiling down and walking with me every step of the way.

Concluding Thoughts and a Discussion of Future Research Possibilities for Graduate Education at HBCUs

Advanced degrees are vehicles for Black students to attain higher income as well as increased social capital (Baum, Ma, & Payea, 2013). Yet, merely gaining access to graduate programs is not enough. Black graduate students have to be properly supported and given adequate financial and social resources to ensure their successes in their graduate programs and beyond. Due to the mission of HBCUs and the uniqueness of a number of their programs, these institutions are well positioned to provide this support to Black graduate students. This volume aids in understanding not only how this support and environment occurs but also aids in a deeper understanding of the experiences of Black students in these programs.

In gaining a deeper understanding of the inner workings, policies, and practices of HBCU graduate programs, the narrative surrounding HBCUs becomes more diverse. Currently, most literature and research regarding HBCU education focuses on undergraduate programs and undergraduate student experiences. In addition, this research is often comparative in nature to PWIs. This current framework is problematic and at its core racially prejudiced. The chapters in this volume, through the power of the narrative, in turn shift the larger HBCU narrative. The volume gives the reader insight into HBCU graduate programs through the authentic lenses and voices of actual members of the HBCU graduate program community. HBCU graduate programs are provided a platform through their own students free of an outside filter. Furthermore, this volume diversifies the narrative around Black graduate students. Literature often narrows Black graduate student voices to a singular expression. In this volume, the prismatic nature of Black graduate students and their experiences is highlighted. This approach fights the tendency to consider the Black graduate student experience as monolithic. All graduate student experiences are unique, and therefore it is important to include a diverse, wide array of student voices when discussing graduate school experiences. As many persons are encouraging students, particularly students of color, to pursue advanced degrees, volumes such as this add to the information and resources that can aid students in selecting what institutional types they would like to attend and graduate experiences they desire to engage.

Graduate school can be a challenging time in one's life, both academically and personally. Furthermore, having a space that culturally supports students can be instrumental in having a positive and successful graduate school experience. For a majority of my doctoral experience at a PWI, I found myself the only Black woman in the department—including faculty. Although I received support from various persons, there were concerns, issues, and experiences that I found myself having to search outside to find support, advice, and Black female mentors. As a Black woman graduate student, having a community that could support me in that process was invaluable. HBCUs tend to have more diverse faculty than their PWI counterparts

(Gasman, Lundy-Wagner, Ransom, & Bowman, 2010; Gasman et al., 2013). Black students who attend HBCUs have a greater chance of not only seeing more faculty of color in their field but also having a mentor and advisor who is also Black. For certain fields of study students may find they are the only Black student in their department. Attending an HBCU not only increases their chances of a diverse cohort and department but also lessens the chance of experiencing isolation.

This volume lays the foundation for future research regarding HBCU graduate programs as well as HBCU graduate student experiences. In learning more about HBCU graduate student experiences, researchers will be able to identify effective practices and policies to be explored in more depth, ultimately adding to various student development and institutional practice theory and literature. Also, as more is learned about graduate students of color, particularly Black men and women, more must be understood regarding how various institutional and program types play a role in those students' academic, professional, economic, and social successes. This volume also gives way to learning more about HBCU graduate programs' relationship with Black students' psychosocial development. HBCUs have played a major role in creating what we deem today as the "Black middle class." However, as the definition of "middle class" begins to shift, this proposition will need to be revisited, along with how HBCUs contribute not merely through undergraduate education but through graduate and professional education as well. Going a step further, more must be understood as to how HBCUs contribute to the building of the overall "middle class," especially when many HBCU graduate programs are more demographically diverse than their PWI counterparts. Last, through students' experiences and perspectives, future researchers can begin to explore institutional decision-making and structures that ultimately have an impact on graduate students. Along with this, researchers can also determine what external factors can affect institutions at large and individual students specifically.

References

Baum, S., Ma, J., & Payea, K. (2013). *Education pays 2013: The benefits of higher education for individuals and society*. New York: The College Board.

Conrad, C. F., Brier, E. M., & Braxton, J. (1997). Factors contributing to the matriculation of White students in public HBCUs. *Journal for a Just and Caring Education, 3*(1), 37–62.

Fountaine, T. P. (2008). *African American voices and doctoral education at HBCUs: Experiences, finances, and agency*. (Doctoral Dissertation, Morgan State University, 2008).

Gasman, M., Lundy-Wagner, V., Ransom, T., & Bowman, N. (2010). *Unearthing promise and potential: Our nation's historically Black colleges and universities*. San Francisco, CA: Jossey-Bass.

Gasman, M., Nguyen, T., Castro Samayoa, A., Commodore, F., Abiola, U., Hyde-Carter, Y., & Carter, C. (2013). *The changing face of historically Black colleges and universities*. Philadelphia: University of Pennsylvania, Center for Minority Serving Institutions.

Gasman, M., & Williams, M. S. (2012). A story history of graduate and professional programs at historically Black colleges and universities. In R. T. Palmer, A. A. Hilton, & T. P. Fountaine (Eds.), *Black graduate education at historically Black colleges and universities: Trends, experiences, and outcomes* (pp. 9–24). New York/London: Information Age Press.

Hale, F. W. (2006). *How Black colleges empower Black students: Lessons for higher education*. Sterling, VA: Stylus Publishing.

Lundy-Wagner, V. C. (2012). Contributing beyond the baccalaureate: Graduate and professional degree programs at HBCUs. In R. T. Palmer, A. A. Hilton, & T. P. Fountaine (Eds.), *Black graduate education at historically Black colleges and universities: Trends, experiences, and outcomes* (pp. 25–40). New York/London: Information Age Press.

Palmer, R. T. (2012). An exploratory study of factors that influence Black students to attend historically Black colleges and universities for graduate school. In R. T. Palmer, A. A. Hilton, & T. P. Fountaine (Eds.), *Black graduate education at historically Black colleges and universities: Trends, experiences, and outcomes* (pp. 41–60). New York/London: Information Age Press.

Palmer, R. T., & Maramba, D. C. (2015a). A delineation of Asian American and Latino/a students' experiences with faculty at an historically Black college and university. *Journal of College Student Development, 56*(2), 111–126.

Palmer, R. T., & Maramba, D. C. (2015b). Racial microaggressions among Asian American and Latino/a students at a historically Black university. *Journal of College Student Development, 56*(7), 705–722.

Perna, L. W. (2001). The contribution of historically Black colleges and universities to the preparation of African Americans for faculty careers. *Research in Higher Education, 42*(3), 567–294.

Provasnik, S., Shafer, L. L., & Snyder, T. (2004). *Historically Black colleges and universities, 1976 to 2001* (NCES 2004–062). U.S. Department of Education, National Center for Education Statistics. Washington, DC: Government Printing Office.

U.S. Commission on Civil Rights. (2010). *The educational effectiveness of historically Black colleges and universities*. Washington, DC: U.S. Commission on Civil Rights. Retrieved from http://www.usccr.gov/pubs/HBCU_webversion2.pdf

2 A Strange Song in a Familiar Land

Lamar Hylton

Choosing to enroll into a doctoral program is often a choice that is accompanied by mixed emotions, arduous decisions, and preparation for a significant lifestyle adjustment. Whereas the thought of attaining the highest level of education in a chosen field of study seems like a grand prize, the process by which this goal is attained is riddled with challenges and unknown circumstances. It is a common thought that the volume of reading and writing, seemingly unending research, and high level of critical thinking and discourse comprise the toughest components of a doctoral program. Yet, there are parts of the process that prove challenging even before a student steps foot into his or her first course. Selecting the right institution to attend, financing the degree, and determining research interests can often add to the complexity and challenge of attaining the doctorate. Such was the case as I embarked upon the journey toward obtaining a PhD. After receiving my bachelor's degree from an historically Black university and my master's degree from a predominately White institution (PWI), I had to make the tough decision of whether to enter a doctoral program. Whereas I knew that my ultimate professional goal of becoming a vice president for student affairs necessitated a terminal degree, I found myself mentally burned out after completing my master's. This, coupled with the fact that I had just started my first professional position in residence life, dissuaded me from wanting to enroll. However, just four short months after completing my master's, I started the process of applying to a doctoral program. In this chapter, I will discuss navigating the application process, my experiences navigating the school I received my undergraduate degree from as a doctoral student, and the impact these experiences have had on my career as a higher education professional.

Fair, Morgan

The lyrics to the alma mater of Morgan State University state "Fair, Morgan, we love thee, so tried and so true. . . ." I embodied my commitment to these words by choosing to attend this institution twice. Morgan State is a historically Black university, located in Baltimore, Maryland. Whereas the standard process of selecting a doctoral program commonly revolves around the strength of the program, how robust the opportunities are to research and publish, and the caliber of faculty members teaching in the program, my decision to attend Morgan State as a doctoral student revolved around three distinct areas: convenience, cost, and familiarity.

Convenience

After graduating with my master's degree, I accepted a live-in position in residence life at a small, private liberal arts college in the suburbs of Baltimore. Whereas it was not my initial intent to enter the field of higher education through residence life, the opportunity to live somewhere where I did not have to pay rent, utilities, and other household bills was very appealing. I decided to take the position because it allowed me to return to Baltimore, where I had made many friends and acquaintances during my time as an undergraduate student. When I made the decision to enter a doctoral program, I knew I needed a program that was geographically convenient to the campus that I lived and worked on due to the nature of my position. As a residence life staff member, there were several times throughout the academic year that I would be on call for campus crises and emergencies. As such, balancing being on call with attending classes would require me to attend an institution that was close to where I lived. Morgan State was just a few minutes from my new home, allowing me to navigate the needs of both my professional and educational pursuits successfully.

Additionally, in the state of Maryland, there are only two brick-and-mortar doctoral programs in higher education administration. The University of Maryland-College Park offers a PhD as well as Morgan State. With the limited options and availability of programs at institutions in Maryland, I was forced to, again, choose a program based on convenience. Whereas the program at the University of Maryland-College Park is certainly revered and highly regarded as one of the premier programs in higher education, the distance from my home and work prevented this program from being an option. Having said that, it is important to note that I did not view the higher education program at Morgan State as a second-tier program to the University of Maryland-College Park. Both programs provided the framework for a quality education replete with opportunities for research, an engaged faculty, and experiences that would afford me the opportunity to be successful as a practitioner. The convenience of access to these programs did, however, play a major role in my selection of a program.

Cost

Another significant factor in my decision-making was the cost of attendance. I had accumulated a significant amount of student loan debt, primarily from my master's program. Because of this, I desired to attend an institution that was affordable and provided a host of options for paying for school, outside of student loans. The total cost of attendance at Morgan State was significantly lower than that of the University of Maryland-College Park. Additionally, Morgan State offered several options for financing a graduate education, including several types of institutional scholarships, fellowships, and grant opportunities. This was in alignment with my experience as an undergraduate where the means of financing my education were also plentiful. Because I was enrolling into the doctoral program as a part-time student, I qualified for scholarship that would cover all of the credit hours I intended to take each semester. Obtaining this scholarship diminished my out-of-pocket expenses significantly and allowed for a more realistic opportunity to achieve the terminal degree.

As a practitioner of higher education, one of the many draws to the field is the ability to finance advanced educational pursuits through the institution you work for. Several of my colleagues in the field work for colleges and universities that will pay a portion of their educational costs through tuition reimbursement, tuition remission, and other programs. Unfortunately, the institution I worked for at the time of my enrollment only paid through the attainment of a master's degree at their institution. This limitation was a significant barrier and caused me to have to be very creative and diligent in finding opportunities to fund my education. The flexible options that Morgan State provided, again, relieved some of this pressure and positioned me to be successful in matriculating through a doctoral program.

Familiarity

Probably the most significant factor in choosing Morgan State for my doctoral pursuit was the familiarity of the institution. Because I had attended and received my undergraduate degree from this institution, there was a sense of comfort in returning to a familiar place. I felt that I would be better suited and more equipped to navigate the culture of the institution, especially after having attended a PWI for my master's degree and realizing the distinct differences in the cultural and political landscapes of each. Additionally, I have a firm belief in the quality of an HBCU education. Society continues to question the relevance and need of HBCUs because many PWIs have increased the educational access and opportunities for Black students over time (Allen, 1992; Fleming, 2001; King, 1993). My decision to attend Morgan State was significantly steeped in the desire to be a living example of how an HBCU education is still relevant and an important vehicle to drive innovation, quality scholarly contribution, and sound expertise in a chosen field of study. As an administrator in higher education, it was my hope to meld my educational experiences at an HBCU with my practical experiences working at PWIs to develop students holistically. By choosing to return to Morgan State to further my education, I felt that I had an upper hand in being able to glean the experiences necessary to accomplish my professional goals without having to experience a significant adjustment to the culture and politics of the institution.

In theory, my desire to champion the political and cultural landmines that exist on any campus, most especially on HBCU campuses, was lofty and seemingly unattainable. However, the reality of my experience was much different. I experienced significant challenges in areas that I felt I should have either anticipated issues to arise or in areas that I felt that I was equipped to tackle challenges because of my history with the institution. These challenges affected my experience as a doctoral student in various, and mostly negative, ways. I found myself having to readjust, refocus, and reexamine my reasoning for attending Morgan State. I had critical questions about whether I was truly equipped to be a doctoral student and whether I had made the right decision to come back to the institution I loved as an undergraduate. There were several moments where I was on the brink of withdrawing from the program and the institution. In short, the Morgan State experience that I thought I knew was very different from what I was experiencing. I found myself singing a strange song in a familiar land.

Singing the Strange Song

During my first semester of the program, I recall attending a panel discussion about how to successfully navigate the doctoral program. The panel was comprised of a few doctoral candidates and some recent graduates of the program. There was one panelist who, when asked what advice she would give those students who were just embarking on their doctoral journey, answered by saying, "A PhD or EdD is much more than just a degree. The doctoral degree is a lifestyle. You have to be ready to live the life or else you will not be successful on the journey." In that moment, I did not fully understand what she meant. My basic recipe for success in the program was simply go to class, read the required literature, write the requisite papers, defend my dissertation, and graduate. Little did I realize that the advice imparted by the wise recent alumna on the panel would ring true through the duration of my time as a student.

Navigating Self-Doubt

As an undergraduate student at Morgan State, I found myself surrounded by the most nurturing and supportive faculty members. I was a music major, and most of the faculty in my major taught courses in each year of my matriculation. This allowed them to understand my strengths and weaknesses and for us to build meaningful relationships with each other. Scholars have often posited that the frequency and quality of student-faculty interactions have significant impact on student retention and progression to degree completion (Kim & Sax, 2009; Kuh & Hu, 2001; Sax, Bryant, & Harper, 2005). Certainly, this was the case for me. I attribute much of my success to the high-quality interactions with my undergraduate faculty. As a result of my positive interactions with my undergraduate faculty, I expected my interactions to be similar as a doctoral student. After all, I was at the same institution so there should certainly be some commonality to how faculty approached their interactions with students regardless of their classification. However, I found the interactions to be quite different in my doctoral work.

It was not that the faculty were not still nurturing as was the case with Morgan's undergraduate faculty. I still felt that the faculty members in the higher education program cared about the success of all of their students. The difference between the two was doctoral faculty nurtured us, as students, very differently. The faculty asked thought-provoking and critical questions related to the lifestyle of a doctoral student. How did we know that we were ready for this journey? In what ways would we contribute to the body of research? I distinctly remember sitting in a statistics course my first semester in the program. The faculty member had a very no-nonsense approach to teaching statistics. When asked why she was "so tough" on us as first-year students, her reply was simple, yet powerful. She informed us that, beyond the knowledge of statistical analyses, if we had not critically examined our propensity to navigate the journey toward the doctorate, we were missing the mark. She went on to say that, whereas many people in society had a doctoral degree, not everyone with a doctorate was "her colleague." In order to rise to the level of colleague, one would have to know much more than what the textbook taught. I remember that, by the end of her impassioned speech, two of my classmates were in tears. I left that class with a lot of doubt about whether I would be able to survive this journey and whether I had made the right choice by enrolling. I was also very conflicted, feeling that the nurturing Morgan State that I once knew had turned cold and heartless.

After several days of pondering that experience in my statistics class, I had a conversation with my adviser. I shared with my adviser what happened in the class and how I had a lot of doubts and questions about my ability to survive the program. I also shared my concerns about how it seemed that the faculty member did not care about the students' success. I questioned how it could be that this faculty member was there to ensure that each student was successful in passing this course but made it extremely difficult to do so and offered no support or encouragement to students who were struggling in her class. My adviser responded by saying that a part of the role of the faculty in a doctoral program was to develop and sharpen students' critical thinking skills and to challenge them to think deeply about their own worldviews in relationship to the study of the student's discipline. By examining the lenses that I looked at the world through, I would be poised to navigate the doctoral program successfully. In order to get to this level of critical examination, it was important for faculty to ask deep and probing questions that are sometimes uncomfortable to think about. As a student, it would be in my best interest to learn how to become comfortable being uncomfortable. I needed to reframe how I thought about critical feedback from faculty members. Instead of taking what faculty members say as them not caring about the success of a student, see their commentary as them seeing something in you that you have not yet seen in yourself and challenging you to think deeply about it. Suffice it to say that, after this conversation with my adviser, I realized that the faculty of this program did, indeed, care. I was also able to reflect on these words and use them to navigate moments of self-doubt throughout my time as a doctoral student.

Cultivating University Pride

As a student of an HBCU, the development of university pride is instilled in myriad ways. Attending sporting events, participating in homecoming festivities, and joining a Greek letter organization are some ways that pride is cultivated among students at HBCUs. Certainly, I entered the doctoral program with an already developed pride about the institution I was attending. Whereas many of my classmates had pride in their respective undergraduate institutions, I felt it was my duty to make sure that my peers knew Morgan State University was the premier place to be. The pride I felt as an undergraduate and alumnus spilled over into my time pursing an advanced degree. I assumed that my fellow doctoral colleagues would develop that same pride that I felt, even if they graduated from other institutions. As we progressed through our journey in the doctoral program, I realized that the university pride I felt as an undergraduate was on a different level than during my time as a doctoral student. I found myself being less prideful about the opportunities to join with and engage in campus activities and more prideful about the work my institution was doing to cultivate Black scholars. Additionally, the peer circle I developed in the program further fueled my pride. To be surrounded by men and women who had significant academic prowess and practical experiences in higher education was both motivating and inspiring. The myriad opportunities to engage in critical discourse and meaningful research with my peers affirmed for me that I had made an excellent decision to attend Morgan State. I found myself prideful that my institution was sending high-caliber scholars into the field to make significant and meaningful contributions to our field. I took pride in the opportunity to contribute to a narrative that challenged the notion that the relevance of an HBCU education is devalued and diminished. The scholarly activity that we participated in as students enhanced my already existing pride in my institution.

My pride in the university manifested in a variety of ways. I was always seizing opportunities to serve on panels, lead discussions, and participate in activities that allowed me the opportunity to share my story with others. I had a keen interest in sharing this story with budding doctoral students who were either thinking of enrolling or within the first year of their enrollment into the program. My adviser was good about positioning me to present and share with various groups about my Morgan journey. Whereas these types of opportunities were abundant for me, I was not naïve enough to believe that the same would be true for everyone in the program. There were peers of mine who had a very difficult time finding engagement opportunities to display what they were learning and how they were developing in the program. I considered myself very blessed to have the opportunities to engage in the ways that I did. Not only was I continually cultivating my presentation and public speaking skills—skills that would be critical to my success when it was time to defend my dissertation—but I was also able to affirm my experience at Morgan State and to, hopefully, impart wisdom that would inspire others to own the lifestyle of a doctoral student.

From Student to Scholar

The fundamental framing of a doctoral program is to equip students to become scholars. Studies show that only 2 percent of Americans have an earned doctorate (U.S. Census Bureau, 2012). My belief is that this low percentage is alarming and also speaks to the strong academic rigor that a doctoral program provides. Reflecting on my experience in the program, I can honestly say that I can concretely note my transformation from novice student to budding scholar. In comparison to my experience as an undergraduate student, the doctoral journey was replete with moments that shifted my approach to inquiry and my questioning of college and university systems and structures. I cannot say that I noticed this transformation while navigating the doctoral process. It was not until after I graduated that I realized that I was, for all intents and purposes, a different person from when I started. This was largely shown through the development of my critical thinking skills and the ability to apply those skills to all aspects of my life, including my educational pursuits. For me, the higher education administration program at Morgan State gave me the tools necessary to be an effective practitioner and a sound researcher. Whereas the grit of pursuing a doctoral degree was often daunting, I emerged ready to seize my professional pursuits with confidence in my ability to translate theory to practice. This confidence is largely attributed to the experiences, lessons learned, and values clarified while living the lifestyle of a Morgan State doctoral student.

Setup for Success

Since entering the field of higher education as a practitioner, I have been afforded many opportunities to advance and further develop my career and professional development. Currently serving as a senior student affairs leader at a large, public research university, I would have never imagined achieving this level of professional success in such a quick amount of time.

As I have ascended the ranks of the proverbial career ladder, there are several lessons that I learned that have contributed to my success.

Believe in Yourself

As mentioned previously, I had to navigate and negotiate high levels of self-doubt throughout my journey as a doctoral student. I have also had to deal with self-doubt in my professional career. There were times where I did not feel that I was adequately prepared to take on the next level in my career. I recall applying for my first director-level position at a small, public liberal arts university in the South. The position involved leading an entire functional area that I had only had indirect experiences in. I remember feeling very excited about the opportunities the position would afford the selected candidate but also feeling like there was no way that I would be successful in obtaining it, based on my qualifications. After doing some soul searching and praying, I remembered the words of my doctoral adviser. I had to push myself beyond the boundaries of my comfort zone and realize that there were strong qualities within me that I had to believe in for myself before I could expect anyone else to believe in me. I applied to the position and emerged as the top candidate for the job. I have found the lessons on self-doubt that I learned while matriculating through the doctoral program have been applicable in my professional journey as well.

Seize the Moment

In each of my professional positions, there have been opportunities that have presented themselves that have contributed significantly to my holistic professional development. In each of those moments, it was important to be timely and firm in my quest to position myself for strategic career advancement. In other words, seizing the moment was of great importance. This was yet another skill that was sharpened during my time as a doctoral student. A mentor of mine once advised me to make sure that I was taking advantage of every opportunity that came my way. Looking back, I can say that Morgan State equipped me to do just that, both as an undergraduate and as a doctoral student. Seizing each moment has catapulted my career in ways unimaginable. For example, my current position was newly created and developed with me in mind. I received a phone call from a friend and mentor in the field who said she was creating this senior-level student affairs position and wanted me to apply for it. Although I was happy in the position I was in at the time, I knew I needed to seize this opportunity to advance my career. The decision to assume my current professional responsibilities was not an easy one to make. Yet I found comfort and peace in knowing that opportunities like this did not come along often and I needed to take advantage of them when they did come. I remembered being eager in my doctoral program to tell the story of my experience at Morgan State through panel discussions and other avenues. The same eagerness rang true for my professional development. These moments gave me the opportunity to tell my story through my work ethic and leadership skills.

Advice for Aspiring Doctoral Students

The decision to enroll into a doctoral program is one that is rewarding and filled with many emotions. Enrolling at an HBCU adds an additional layer of excitement and challenge as the process of matriculating at an historically Black institution is very unique from other types of colleges and universities. As the process begins to unfold, it is important to realize that patience is a key virtue. Throughout the process, from applying to defending the dissertation, there will be much information to absorb and myriad concepts to learn. It is vitally important to ensure that aspirants remain patient with themselves and others as they go through. It can be very easy to want to get to the finish line—the defense of the dissertation—very quickly. However, it is essential that time is taken to navigate the institutional culture and learn the lessons necessary to achieve ultimate success. Additionally, at an HBCU, it is equally important to understand that the relationships and networks that are established are also important to develop. It will be these relationships that can jumpstart your career.

In addition to the practical advice given to navigate the doctoral journey at an HBCU, it is also crucial to understand that the value of an HBCU education remains worthwhile. As mentioned before, the relevance and worth of historically Black institutions is constantly questioned and scrutinized. There are many who argue that students receive a diluted educational experience by attending an HBCU. As we move toward a more multicultural and diverse society, there are those who feel that HBCUs and other minority-serving institutions are exclusionary and do not provide students the opportunity to explore the richness and fullness of diverse experiences. This is simply untrue and unfounded. On the contrary, an HBCU experience allows students to gain critical insight on issues that affect the Black community as well as society as a whole. The deficit mind-set regarding the value and worth of an HBCU education will continue to further marginalize people of color as a whole. It is very important for those who enroll into doctoral programs at HBCUs to challenge and control the narrative around what the HBCU education really provides. Future scholars must position their research and practical experiences in such a way that provides real-life examples of the worth of being educated at any of these fine institutions. We must know our worth and stand ready to clearly articulate that worth to those who try to misrepresent the experience and quality of an HBCU education.

Finally, as the doctoral journey begins, remember the wise words of the panelist during my first semester in the higher education program. The doctoral degree is much more than just a degree. You must be ready to assume the lifestyle that comes along with being a doctoral student. Sometimes adjusting to this lifestyle is very uncomfortable and often comes with significant challenges. Yet, the adjustment is necessary and essential to success. Do not get so caught up in the perceived glamour of having a doctorate that you miss the opportunity to proactively prepare the lifestyle adjustment that is necessary to achieve the doctorate. It is important that scholars prepare themselves academically, professionally, and personally to embrace the arduous, yet rewarding journey of a doctoral student. Once that lifestyle adjustment is made, success is eminent and fully achievable.

References

Allen, W. R. (1992). The color of success: African American college student outcomes at predominantly White and historically Black colleges and universities. *Harvard Educational Review, 62*(1), 26–44.

Fleming, J. (2001). The impact of a historically Black college on African American students: The case of LeMoyne-Owen College. *Urban Education, 36*(5), 597–610.

Kim, Y. K., & Sax, L. J. (2009). Student-faculty interaction in research universities: Differences by student gender, race, social class, and first-generation status. *Research in Higher Education, 50*(5), 437–459.

King, S. H. (1993). The limited presence of African-American teachers. *Review of Educational Research, 63*(2), 115–149.

Kuh, G. D., & Hu, S. (2001). The effects of student-faculty interaction in the 1990s. *The Review of Higher Education, 24*(3), 309–332.

Sax, L. J., Bryant, A. N., & Harper, C. E. (2005). The differential effects of student-faculty interaction on college outcomes for women and men. *Journal of College Student Development, 50*(6), 642–657.

U.S. Census Bureau. (2012). Most children younger than age 1 are minorities, Census Bureau reports. Retrieved from http://www.census.gov/newsroom/releases/archives/population/cb1290.html

3 Journey to the PhD
A Personal Narrative of Doctoral Studies at an HBCU

Tiffany F. Boykin

Although considerable information pertaining to graduate education has been compiled in national databases, and there have been several studies related to Black doctoral education, there has been limited research dedicated exclusively to the ways in which Black students describe their doctoral experiences, especially at historically Black colleges and universities (HBCUs). In addition, few studies have determined which factors influence the HBCU doctoral experience and shape the doctoral socialization process for Black students. The goal of this chapter is to present a personal narrative cataloguing my motivation for attending an HBCU for doctoral study, my overall matriculation experiences, and how those experiences have shaped my career as a higher education practitioner and scholar. It is hoped that this personal journey will help to address continued inadequacies in the literature and to contribute to a framework for faculty, administrators, and students alike to assess HBCU doctoral program development and inform practice.

Motivating Factors for "Girls Like Me"

There is a plethora of literature on higher education school choice, particularly outlining which factors drive an individual student to pursue postsecondary studies and which factors are influential to a student's selection of one institution over another (Cabrera & La Nasa, 2002; Mattern & Wyatt, 2009; Perez & McDonough, 2008; Pitre, 2006). The literature has suggested that motivating factors for postsecondary school choice includes salience and relevance (Walker, 2008), benefits, rewards, and assumed payoffs related to college choice (Beattie, 2002), emotion and brand loyalty (Kirp, 2003), the role of parents (Rowan-Kenyon, Bell, & Perna, 2008), high school counselors (McDonough, 2005; Perna et al., 2008), secondary teachers (Croninger & Lee, 2001; Johnson, Rochkind, Ott, & DuPont; 2010), and peers (Fletcher, 2010). In terms of graduate programs, additional factors include financial aid (Mertz, Strayhorn, & Eckman, 2012), location and flexibility of program (Talbot, Maier, & Rushlau, 1996), institutional reputation

(Mertz & McNeely, 1989), personal contact with the faculty, and a recommendation from a significant other (Olson, 1992). And when it comes to students choosing an HBCU, researchers have concluded that academics, finances, geography, and social life (Van Camp, Barden, Sloan, & Clarke, 2009); positive student-faculty interactions (Berger & Milem, 2000); and an increased feeling of belonging and pride (Freeman, 2005; Nora, 2004) are influential.

Notwithstanding, there remain some gaps in our understanding of what other motivational factors are at play when students are making the critical decision as to what institution they will entrust to nurture them during the arduous process of doctoral study. Whereas some students are very intentional about their college choice decisions and can point to specific components of the choice process, such as an institution's program offerings or the financial aid package, others may have come to the HBCU by chance and based upon much deeper but often undefined interactions. Before I can share my specific motives for choosing an HBCU, it is important to provide a context for the decision-making space I found myself in when it was time to choose. The following is an excerpt from unpublished comments that I made during an acceptance speech for a professional award. The closing comments reflect and appropriately contextualize where I was at the time of initiating the institution selection process for doctoral study.

> *It is my honor to stand before such distinguished colleagues, mentors, committee members, and other supporters to accept the 2011 Carlos J. Vallejo Memorial Award for Emerging Scholarship. I was absolutely thrilled when I learned that I had been nominated for this award . . . As I processed what I wanted to share with you briefly this evening, one critical aspect of education rested heavily on my mind. That aspect is the issue of access and participation in higher education for racial and ethnic minorities, particularly the process and journey associated with graduate education for Black students and the role of historically black colleges and universities or HBCUs. That process and journey have had a profound influence and have been critical in shaping the practitioner and emerging scholar that stands before you today . . . Before I close, I'd like to take a few moments to share a personal story with you—one that might better explain why that graduate process I spoke about earlier is so very meaningful for me and why I believe it critically shaped the practitioner-scholar that I am today. When I was pursuing a master's degree, I was one of two Black students in the entire program at a predominately White institution. I often felt that sense of isolation, disconnect, responsibility for the Black race, and other characteristics that I would later learn are indicative to some minority student experiences on predominantly White campuses. Those feelings came to a climax at the end of my last semester as I was preparing to defend my master's thesis. I began seriously considering pursuing a PhD and requested letters of recommendation from known and*

trusted faculty members. One faculty member concluded and very clearly articulated to me that she was not supportive of my PhD goal. She indicated that my work was inferior and not worthy of graduate study. In fact, she was unsure as to how I'd even made it that far. She went on to exclaim, "You shouldn't even be thinking about a PhD; you'll never get accepted into any doctoral program." Needless to say I left her office that day feeling quite defeated and very low.

I talked to my thesis advisor who told me not worry. She explained that the particular faculty member was tired, under lots of pressure, and just wasn't used to working with "girls like me." My advisor meant well, but I couldn't help but wonder what exactly did she mean by "girls like me." She went on to explain that "girls like me" were considered academically underprepared for graduate study, often came from underserved communities, and were part of underrepresented populations. I thought to myself, wow, that's a lot of "UNDER." My advisor also went on to explain that Dr. "BadMentor" simply didn't have a lot of connection with urban minority students. Well, I didn't UNDERstand any of it. Was this who I was? The totality of my academic being and potential rest in the fact that I was academically underprepared (allegedly), underserved, and underrepresented? THAT was me? Needless to say, I felt like crawling UNDER a rock.

I never did find that rock to crawl under, but I did stumble upon a rock to lean on—a wonderful institution known as Morgan State University. This historically Black university welcomed a "girl like me." In that space, I was exposed to the teachings, mentorship, and interactions with a dynamic faculty who made efforts to ensure my academic experiences were intellectually stimulating, engaging, and culturally relevant—something I didn't even know existed. At Morgan State, "girls like me" were not simply characterized as underprepared, underserved, underrepresented, urban, or any other pre-entry circumstance that may have outfitted their admission application. At Morgan State, "girls like me" were encouraged and empowered, supported, and developed. The expectations were high and the work was rigorous! At Morgan State, "girls like me" earned a PhD in higher education and graduated with a 4.00 cumulative GPA.

The aforementioned comments were made well after I had selected an HBCU for doctoral study. In fact, they were made well after I had earned my doctorate. But when it was time to choose an institution for doctoral study, those comments captured the essence of where I was emotionally. I vividly recall making application to several programs at PWIs; I had not even considered an HBCU for many reasons, some of which I will discuss later in the recommendations section in this chapter. I was not admitted to any of the institutions to which I had applied and had begun to not only acknowledge those allegations of Dr. "BadMentor," but I had even begun to internalize them.

On a crisp spring day, I made my way to the School of Graduate Studies at Morgan State University and had a chance, but very engaging encounter, with a doctoral student in the higher education program. I asked a few questions, gathered a few brochures, and arranged a time to meet with the program coordinator later that day. I eventually met with the coordinator, a distinguished faculty member from the department. By the close of that conversation, I knew that Morgan State University was the place for me. I walked in feeling very inadequate and doubtful of my potential for success in a PhD program. But I left feeling empowered, and while still doubtful in some ways, eager to know more and to learn more. In just that short time, I would experience just a snapshot of the nurturing and engaging interaction between faculty and student that I would later learn was so unique to the HBCU experience and highly associated with HBCU doctoral student success. In that short time, I would participate in a supportive and engaging encounter with a peer—another characteristic that I would also later learn is associated with HBCU doctoral student success. In that short time, I would gain the courage and audacity needed to not only counter Dr. "BadMentor's" narrative, but begin the work toward becoming a change agent and social engineer for "girls like me." It was in those experiences, albeit brief, that I can point to the true motivating factors for my selecting an HBCU for doctoral study.

On the Road to PhD: Reflecting on My Socialization at an HBCU

In general, socialization has been characterized as a broad concept in higher education, which has been extensively applied and conceptualized within graduate study to primarily understand student development and attrition (Gardner, 2008; Golde, 1998; Lovitts, 2001; Weidman, Twale, & Stein, 2001). Some scholars have identified the academic department or discipline as the principal site of graduate student socialization (Gardner, 2007; Golde, 1998), due in large part to departmental power over admissions, funding, and degree requirements influenced by disciplinary norms and practices (Golde, 2005). Other researchers have added that socialization also tends to occur in the cultures of "graduate education, its values, and tenets across institutions and disciplines" and "institutional culture, which includes general norms and procedures governing the day-to-day working of the graduate enterprise" (Gardner, 2007, p. 737).

Another perspective of doctoral student socialization draws from Baird's (1993) integrated model for student development. This model described the doctoral experience as a process of socialization to an ultimate professional role. This role, according to Baird (1993), involves learning the specialized knowledge, skills, attitudes, values, norms, and interests of the profession. In this model, graduate faculty members are considered a critical agent for conducting doctoral student socialization because faculty members define knowledge and disciplinary values. Faculty members model the roles of academics in the discipline and provide practical help and advice. In addition, according to Baird (1993), the other socialization agents, who have rarely been formally recognized, are graduate students' peers.

A clear deficit in the doctoral student socialization literature is that fact that, overall, little attention has been given to how minority, particularly Black, doctoral students are socialized. Although disproportionate completion rates for minorities pursuing doctorates has prompted some doctoral education researchers to examine the socialization experiences of these students (Bowen & Rudenstine, 1992; Golde & Walker, 2006; Lovitts, 2001; Pauley, Cunningham, & Toth, 1999), the work lacks in-depth consideration of specific models of leadership and socialization as it relates to Black success at the doctoral level (Felder, 2015). Moreover, even less consideration has been made for examining the socialization experiences of Black doctoral students attending HBCUs (Fountaine, 2012).

As I reflect on my doctoral student experiences at Morgan State, considering both challenges and successes, three aspects of the socialization process are salient for me: (1) institutional and program related pre-entry experiences, and concepts of (2) faculty agency and (3) peer agency. Each component played a role during my tenure Morgan State and is equally considered as I attempt to articulate and best capture my experiences during doctoral study.

Pre-Entry Experiences

Historically, researchers have found a positive link between students' pre-entry experiences and their overall experience matriculating through academic programs (Bowman, 2005; Tinto, 1975). In a quantitative investigation examining the experience of Black doctoral students at HBCUs, pre-entry experience—a student's level of awareness and understanding of program requirements and expectations prior to being admitted to a program—was revealed as a best predictor for a satisfying doctoral experience and perceived persistence, or strong belief the student would successfully complete doctoral study (Fountaine, 2008).

In my personal pursuit of the PhD at an HBCU, institutional and program related pre-entry experiences were indeed an important aspect of my overall doctoral student experience. Researchers have concluded that relatively low numbers of graduate students were well informed about the nature of graduate study or what would be expected of them (Lovitts & Nelson, 2000). Likewise, Golde and Dore (2001) revealed a statistically significant number of students did not clearly understand what doctoral study entailed, how the process worked, and how to navigate it effectively. I too did not have a full appreciation for the nature of doctoral study or what doctoral study would entail. Because of my insufficient understanding of the process, I did experience some dissonance, even in the most supportive and encouraging environment of an HBCU. In those first few classes, it appeared that everyone seemed to be so learned in the discipline, and they all seemed to have a solid grasp and conceptualization of the dissertation process, including having identified a research topic. I was lost, but not hopeless. I had experienced a sense of being lost before in my master's program, but this time around, I felt as if there were people in place who were willing and able to show me the way. Soon, I was able to navigate the subsequent doctoral processes and coursework effectively by taking initiative to inquire about program norms and culture. In addition, I received reinforced support from peers and faculty to mitigate the learning curve associated with newer doctoral students.

Faculty Agency

The literature has confirmed that faculty agency, or faculty-student interaction, has played a critical role in the socialization process and academic success of graduate students (Baird, 1993). This sentiment is not new as Arce and Manning (1984) and Blackwell (1987) found that graduate students perceived the relationships with faculty and mentors as critical to their satisfaction and successful completion of graduate programs. Particularly relevant to my journey, researchers have found that one of the major socializing agents of graduate students on private Black campuses was indeed the faculty and staff (Latiker, 2003).

Whereas pre-entry experience, peer agency, and faculty agency share equally significant roles in doctoral student experiences, faculty agency, conceptualized as faculty-student engagement through interaction, was the most influential in my personal journey. I liken my experience to the outcomes in a study investigating the experience of Black doctoral students at HBCUs (Fountaine, 2008). In that investigation, three types of engagement were significant to Black doctoral students' positive experiences: (1) internal engagement, (2) external engagement, and (3) adviser engagement. Internal engagement was defined as the involvement between a student and an adviser with regard to academic program progress and research practices. External engagement concerned the social components for student success that were external to a student's program and research practices, such as the development of survival skills for the field of study and information about career paths. Adviser engagement measured the overall interaction between a doctoral student and her adviser.

I recall having significantly strong connections with classroom faculty, and particularly with my program adviser and dissertation adviser. I was extremely pleased with my faculty adviser and with the amount and quality of time she spent with me both in and outside of the classroom. The same holds true for my dissertation adviser, who spent an inordinate amount of time coaching, guiding, and supporting me, not just through the dissertation process but through navigating coursework and gateway doctoral activities, such as the comprehensive exam. In addition, he consistently inquired about my personal goals and offered strategies for achieving professional objectives. At Morgan State, faculty demonstrated a genuine caring ethos. They were authentic in their delivery of instruction, as well as their support for my academic success and overall well-being. They were deliberate and intentional about my personal and professional development, and I consistently felt motivated and empowered to achieve. Faculty aided me in refining, and sometimes redefining, professional goals and objectives and helped me to make meaning of course and program content within a much broader context than I ever anticipated. I give substantial credit to the committed and dedicated faculty at Morgan State University for my overall positive doctoral experience and subsequent successful completion.

Peer Agency

At the graduate level, interaction among students and their peers has been recognized as a crucial factor to Black participation in doctoral education (King & Chepyator-Thomson, 1996). Cesari (1990) suggested peer relationships were an important source of support and encouragement for doctoral students and concluded students relied on each other for guidance and knowledge, and they also gained competence and a sense of self-worth by assisting their peers. Similarly, Keintz (1999) consistently listed peers as the individuals who had the greatest impact on student learning and development.

The above-mentioned notions reported in the literature rang true for my journey as well. Early on, I was a bit indifferent and failed to fully invest in peer relationships. However, through the encouragement of faculty and advanced doctoral students (students in their second and third year of study), I soon realized the importance and value of my peers. Group projects, requiring team input and support, enforced the need to capitalize on the diversity of strengths and perspectives of my academic colleagues. Although I did not matriculate in a formal cohort-style model for doctoral study, we began to share the learning experience—the good and the bad—much like a cohort. We saw each other as teacher and learner. In addition, I developed strong bonds, almost family-like, with my peers, and those bonds have lasted well beyond doctoral study and have helped my career development and professional advancement in noteworthy ways.

The HBCU and Achieving Career Objectives

When I began doctoral study, the higher education program at Morgan State University was "designed to develop scholars and practitioners who will improve the world of postsecondary education, as academic leaders, public policy experts, administrators, members of the professoriate, consultants, or training and development professionals. The program is a learning community characterized by scholarly rigor, strong connections to broader communities of practice, and a passion for contributing to the betterment of society through education" (Morgan State University, 2005). I remember my career objectives included goals of being each and every one of the designated roles for which the program was designed to prepare me. I like to think I was ambitious; I now realize that I simply hadn't refined my thought process about my future. Nonetheless, I completed the program with long-term research and practice goals. Essentially, I knew I wanted to develop a career that allowed me to continue to conduct original research and remain directly engaged with students, in a teaching or an administrative capacity. I am pleased to say that I have enjoyed success in both realms and that my doctoral experience at Morgan State University has been a key factor in shaping the scholar-practitioner I am today.

As a Researcher

Much of my research agenda has included examinations of Black doctoral students, particularly at HBCUs. In fact, my personal doctoral journey has been the major impetus to my line of research inquiry. Black doctoral enrollment has shown solid improvement over the last three decades, and the number of Black doctorate recipients currently stands at one of the highest levels in history, with Blacks comprising 6.3 percent of all doctorates awarded to American citizens (National Opinion Research Center [NORC], 2007). Moreover, the role of HBCUs in graduate education has been equally impressive as they have been a critical force in graduate and first professional degree attainment for Black students (St. John, 2000).

As my doctoral student journey was coming to an end, I recognized that Blacks had made notable progress in earning doctorates. However, I knew then that optimism for the future was premature. Whereas there had been considerable data collected on graduate student outcomes, oftentimes the data were collected at the aggregate levels without singling out the accomplishments of doctoral students versus master's students. In addition, very few studies had focused on factors influencing the experiences and persistence for doctoral students, and even fewer had examined those factors for Black students (Nettles & Millet, 2006). That was the case then and remains an issue now. An in-depth understanding of the role HBCUs have on doctoral student success has been somewhat left out of the higher education portrait.

Beyond basic enrollment trends and degree attainment outcomes, we still know very little about how Black students experience doctoral study at HBCUs. My interest in this area of research peaked during my time at Morgan State University as a doctoral student. I understood that my experience was invaluable and wanted to learn more about the experiences of others. During my doctoral studies, I also acknowledged critics who questioned, and still do, the relevancy and continued need for HBCUs (Fryer & Greenstone, 2007; Sowell, 2006). I knew that I wanted to create a research agenda that addressed the inadequacies in the literature and served as a counterargument to critics.

Thus far, my findings suggest that Black doctoral students have better experiences and are more likely to believe they will persist in completing their degrees when they are highly involved with faculty regarding their academic program progress and research practices, when they have high levels of interpersonal interaction with faculty, and when they are actively engaged with faculty about social components external to their academic program. With this in mind, I have made a habit of regularly meeting with my research advisees, in small groups and individually. This is not only to talk about their respective performances but to also gain a sense of how they see themselves progressing and persisting. I model the guidance style of my dissertation chair as I guide others in exploring research ideas and writing the dissertation. In other instances, I challenge students to search for opportunities to make scholarly presentations at regional and national professional conferences. This, too, is a strategy that I modeled from faculty at Morgan State. In general, I purposely position myself as a mentor and encourage students to approach me about their learning needs.

As a Faculty Member

My teaching and administrative philosophy has been most profoundly shaped by graduate student experiences, especially my doctoral experience at Morgan State. My first teaching experiences were with adult learners in a community college setting. Oftentimes, my students were years removed from school or in some extreme cases, had never come into contact with academic rigor. For some teachers, the temptation may have been to diminish the academic demands. However, due in large part to my interactions with faculty in my doctoral program, I made strong efforts to resist that temptation in every class that I taught. I was very deliberate in my assumption that any student was capable of managing the most complex and difficult intellectual concepts. I held high expectations for my students, and they met each and every last one of them. My doctoral experiences helped me to better understand how much teaching and learning is a reciprocal process. My approach has been to always consider the fact that I have as much to learn from my students as they have to learn from me—a consideration to which I was first introduced at Morgan State University.

As I recall, some of the best classes at Morgan State were those in which the faculty were not afraid to take responsibility for their materials and not afraid to admit the limitations of the literature. I was excited to have professors who would challenge and empower students to raise objections, question, critique, and in essence, begin to deconstruct some of the purported "facts," especially with regard to historically marginalized and under-voiced populations. I still wonder to what extent an educator is able to cultivate critical thinking skills in students if she does not enter the class prepared to make determinations, to justify her judgments and perspectives, and to invite students' critiques. In general, I want to provoke my students to think differently, as my HBCU faculty and administrators did for me. I want them to see that the issues that concern us in a specific theory or research methods class are not completely insulated to that class but engage questions and have implications for the world at large. I want to continue to proactively communicate high expectations for success and identify and implement ways for individual students to meet those expectations. Essentially, I want to exhibit the ethic of care and teaching excellence that was shown to me as I pursued my doctorate.

Recommendations for Prospective Doctoral Attendees

In the past, I've often been met with, "Why did you choose an HBCU for doctoral study?" It's not like I had any family, role models, or significant others to promote my attending an HBCU. In fact, I was a first-generation college student who had attended predominantly White institutions for undergraduate and master's studies. To be honest, prior to attending Morgan State University, I had never set foot on an HBCU campus. So when asked about my choice of institution for doctoral study, I often responded with a sincere defense. That is, I would immediately begin to address, and even remedy, all of the challenges associated with attending and earning an advanced degree from an HBCU. During my time at Morgan State University, and even before pursuing doctoral study, I had been well aware of criticisms, which I learned later were often unfounded, and blatant attacks on these unique institutions. For example, HBCU critics have reported that today's graduates of HBCUs receive far less value for their degrees than preceding generations (Fryer & Greenstone, 2007). Further, in a scathing commentary, Riley (2010) asserted that HBCUs are academically inferior and are inferior in preparing students for post-college life. He even suggested that HBCUs might serve higher education better by repurposing themselves as community colleges that focus on developmental courses to compensate for the poor elementary and secondary education that so many Black children receive. Researchers have reported that such widespread notions of inferiority permeate the ways in which students and professionals alike conceptualize the utility and relevance of HBCUs. In turn, many students, professionals, and even those who consider themselves progressive thinkers have continued, sometimes inadvertently, to fuel the misconception that an HBCU education is simply subpar (Barbosa, 2015). At one point, I even found myself defending the many ways *my* institution was not like the HBCUs described by critics. I exclaimed that even if *my* institution was at one time subpar, it had gone above and beyond to remedy all that the critics saw wrong with it.

Through my doctoral studies at Morgan State University, I strengthened my critical thinking competencies and began to challenge others' truth. No longer would I sit back and willingly accept a critic's version of my reality.

The faculty, staff, and peer communities at Morgan State University fostered and supported a mind-set where students felt compelled to be their own fact finders, to question what was put before them, and to deconstruct wide assertions in an effort to expose flaws and gaps that were disadvantageous to an equitable learning process. Today, I am able to offer a strong counter-narrative to the often anecdotal and unfounded assumptions and assertions made by HBCU naysayers. Even when HBCU critics make generalizations based on empirical research, I am able to accurately question their research methodology and heavy reliance on traditional measures of academic excellence. In using a critical lens to scrutinize such works, I have been able to expose flaws in everything from poor research design to poor measures of quality. In fact, it is my opinion that often times critics' assertions about the inferiority of HBCUs have little to do with the quality of the HBCU and more to do with the privilege of its predominately White counterparts.

Today's Black prospective doctoral student has many options for graduate study. And still, the HBCU should warrant strong consideration. HBCUs continue to provide a culturally affirming and psychologically supportive environment for Black doctoral students. They offer a space where students can grow intellectually and celebrate Black cultural heritage and voice. Even in my earliest days of study where I experienced dissonance due to my unfamiliarity with what doctoral study entailed, I never felt as if I didn't belong. HBCU graduate faculty and staff truly value their students and are committed to uncovering and developing potential that has often gone untapped or simply unnoticed in other academic settings. I am a true testament to that fact. For me, doctoral study was a completely different animal from other academic experiences. But for the encouraging and supportive interactions I had with faculty and peers with whom I could identify, I'm not sure I would have successfully earned my doctorate. Professors often went beyond their expected professionally related responsibilities by expressing genuine interest in my development and transformation from student to scholar. At Morgan State University, I was professionally socialized and learned skills and behaviors that would prove impactful long after program completion.

When selecting an institution for doctoral study, Black prospective students should definitely consider the traditional influencers of college choice, such as financial aid and incentives, program reputation and flexibility, and location. Black students should also pay careful attention to opportunities for meaningful engagement and interactions with faculty and peers. Be mindful of the alarming attrition rates for doctoral students across institutions and of the inherent dissonance many students experience as they are unfamiliar with the doctoral study process. Then, students must evaluate the kinds of environments in which they thrive as learners and are best challenged and motivated. Take the time to conduct an introspective inventory of your success needs for doctoral study, beyond that of financial aid and program offerings. It is then that you can make an informed and responsible decision. Perhaps you will join the ranks of myself and countless others. Because of my meaningful and inspiring experiences at Morgan State University, today, when asked why I chose an HBCU for doctoral study, I proudly answer, "Why not?"

References

Arce, C. H., & Manning, W. H. (1984). *Minorities in academic careers: The experiences of Ford Foundation fellows*. New York: Ford Foundation.

Baird, L. L. (1993). Increasing graduate student retention and degree attainment. *New Directions for Institutional Research, 80*, 3–12.

Barbosa, L. (2015). Casual conversations in communicating the value and worth of historically Black colleges and universities. *The Vermont Connection, 32*(2). Retrieved from http://scholarworks.uvm.edu/tvc/vol32/iss1/2

Beattie, I. (2002). Are all "adolescent econometricians" created equal? Racial, class, and gender differences in college enrollment. *Sociology of Education, 75*(1), 19–43.

Berger, J. B., & Milem, J. F. (2000). Exploring the impact of historically Black colleges in promoting the development of undergraduates' self-concept. *Journal of College Student Development, 41*(4), 381–394.

Blackwell, J. E. (1987). *Mainstreaming outsiders: The production of Black professionals* (2nd ed.). Dix Hills, NY: General Hall.

Bowen, W. G., & Rudenstine, N. L. (1992). *In pursuit of the PhD*. Princeton, NJ: Princeton University Press.

Bowman, C. L. (2005). The relationship of pre-enrollment experiences to student fit and college choice. (Doctoral Dissertation, University of Missouri. UMI ProQuest Digital Dissertation, AAT 3235129.

Cabrera, A. F., & La Nasa, S. (2002). Understanding the college choice process. *New Directions for Institutional Research, 2000*(107), 5–22.

Cesari, J. P. (1990). Thesis and dissertation support groups: A unique service for graduate students. *Journal of College Student Development, 31*, 375–378.

Croninger, R. G., & Lee, V. E. (2001). Social capital and dropping out of high school: Benefits to at-risk students of teachers' support and guidance. *Teachers College Record, 103*(4), 548–581.

Felder, P. P. (2015). Edward A. Bouchet: A model for understanding African Americans and their doctoral experience. *Journal of African American Studies, 19*(1), 3–17.

Fletcher, J. M. (2010). *Peer influences on college choices: New evidence from Texas*. New Haven: Yale University.

Fountaine, T. P. (2008). *African American voices and doctoral education at HBCUs: Experiences, finances and agency*. (Doctoral Dissertation, Morgan State University, 2008).

Fountaine, T. P. (2012). Inside Black doctoral education: A quantitative investigation of predictors for engagement and persistence at HBCUs. In R. Palmer, A. Hilton, & T. Fountaine (Eds.), *Black graduate education at historically Black colleges and universities: Trends, experiences, and outcomes* (pp. 133–152). New York/London: Information Age Press.

Freeman, K. (2005). *African Americans and college choice: The influence of family and school*. Albany: State University of New York.

Fryer, R. G., & Greenstone, M. (2007). *The causes and consequences of attending historically Black colleges and universities*. Cambridge, MA: National Bureau of Economic Research.

Gardner, S. K. (2007). "I heard it through the grapevine": Doctoral student socialization in chemistry and history. *Higher Education, 54*(5), 723–740.

Gardner, S. K. (2008). Fitting the mold of graduate school: A qualitative study of socialization in doctoral education. *Innovative Higher Education, 33*(1), 125–138.

Golde, C. M. (1998). Beginning graduate school: Explaining first-year doctoral attrition. In M. S. Anderson (Ed.), *The experience of being in graduate school: An exploration* (pp. 55–64). San Francisco, CA: Jossey-Bass.

Golde, C. M. (2005). The role of the department and discipline in doctoral student attrition: Lessons from four departments. *Journal of Higher Education, 76*(6), 669–700.

Golde, C. M., & Dore, T. M. (2001). *At cross purposes: What the experiences of today's graduate students reveal about doctoral education.* Philadelphia, PA: The Pew Charitable Trusts. Retrieved June 28, 2007 from http://www.phd-survey.org/report%20final.pdf

Golde, C. M., & Walker, G. (Eds.). (2006). *Envisioning the future of doctoral education: Preparing stewards of the discipline.* San Francisco: Jossey-Bass.

Johnson, J., Rochkind, J., Ott, A., & DuPont, S. (2010). *Can I get a little advice here? How an overstretched high school guidance system is undermining students' college aspirations.* New York: Pubic Agenda.

Keintz, B. (1999). Student relationships: An analysis of peer, faculty, and staff effectiveness. *Journal of Student Affairs, 8*(8), 59–70.

King, S. E., & Chepyator-Thomson, J. R. (1996). Factors affecting the enrollment and persistence of African American doctoral students. *Physical Educator, 53*(4), 170–180.

Kirp, D. L. (2003). *Shakespeare, Einstein, and the bottom line: The marketing of higher education.* Cambridge, MA: Harvard University Press.

Latiker, T. T. (2003, April). *A qualitative study of African American student persistence in a private Black college.* Paper presented at the annual meeting of the American Educational Research Association, Chicago, IL. (ERIC Document Reproduction Services No. ED 477 444).

Lovitts, B. E. (2001). *Leaving the ivory tower: The causes and consequences of departure from doctoral study.* Lanham, MD: Rowman & Litttlefield.

Lovitts, B. E., & Nelson, C. (2000). The hidden crisis in graduate education: Attrition from PhD. programs. *Academe, 86*(6), 44–50.

Mattern, K., & Wyatt, J. N. (2009). Student choice of college: How far do students go for an education? *Journal of College Admission, 203*, 18–29.

McDonough, P. M. (2005). Counseling matters: Knowledge, assistance, and organizational commitment in college preparation. In W. G. Tierney, Z. B. Corwin, & J. E. Colyar (Eds.), *Preparing for college: Nine elements of effective outreach* (pp. 69–87). Albany: State University of New York Press.

Mertz, N. T., & McNeely, S. R. (1989, November). *Students' perceptions of their preparation: A focus on departments of educational administration.* Paper presented at the annual meeting of the Southern Regional Council on Educational Administration, Columbia, SC.

Mertz, N. T., Strayhorn, T., & Eckman, E. (2012). Entering student affairs: A comparative study of graduate school choice. *College Student Affairs Journal, 30*(2), 92–93.

Morgan State University. (2005). PhD in higher education administration. Retrieved from http://www.morgan.edu/school_of_education_and_urban_studies/departments/advanced_studies_leadership_and_policy/degreesmajors/higher_education_program_(phd).html

National Opinion Research Center. (2007). *Survey of earned doctorates: Summary report 2006.* Washington, DC: National Academy Press. Retrieved November 23, 2007 from http://www.norc.org/NR/rdonlyres/C22A3F40-0BA2-4993-A6D3-5E65939EEDC3/0/06SRFinalVersion.pdf

Nettles, M. T., & Millet, C. M. (2006). *Three magic words: Getting to PhD*. Baltimore, MD: The Johns Hopkins University Press.

Nora, A. (2004). The role of habitus and cultural capital in choosing a college, transitioning from high school to higher education, and persisting in college among minority and nonminority students. *Journal of Hispanic Higher Education, 3*(2), 180–208.

Olson, C. (1992). Is your institution user-friendly? Essential elements of successful graduate student recruitment. *College and University, 67*(3), 203–214.

Pauley, R., Cunningham, M., & Toth, P. (1999). Doctoral student attrition and retention: A study of a nontraditional Ed.D. program. *Journal of College Student Retention, 1*(3), 225–238.

Perez, P. A., & McDonough, P. M. (2008). Understanding Latino and Latina college choice: A social capital and chain migration analysis. *Journal of Hispanic Higher Education, 7*(3), 249–265. doi: 10.1177/1538192708317620

Perna, L. W., Rowan-Kenyon, H. T., Thomas, S., Bell, A., Anderson, R., & Li, C. (2008). The role of college counseling in shaping college opportunity: Variations across high schools. *Review of Higher Education, 31*(2), 131–159.

Pitre, P. (2006). College choice: A study of African American and White student aspirations related to college attendance. *College Student Journal, 40*(3), 562–574.

Riley, J. (2010, September 28). Black colleges need a new mission. *The Wall Street Journal*. Retrieved from http://www.wsj.com/articles/SB10001424052748704654004575517822124077834

Rowan-Kenyon, H. T., Bell, A., & Perna, L. W. (2008). Contextual influences on parental involvement in college going. *Journal of Higher Education, 79*(5), 564–586.

Sowell, T. (2006). *Choosing a college: A guide for parents and students: An outspoken look at admissions, campus life, and the academic world by a professor and scholar*. Ashland, OR: Blackstone Audio.

St. John, E. (2000, July 6). More doctorates in the house—more African American students are receiving doctorates. *Black Issues in Higher Education*. Retrieved from http://findarticles.com/p/articles/mi_m0DXK/is_10_17/ai_63817017

Talbot, D. M., Maier, E., & Rushlau, M. (1996). Guess who's coming to doctoral programs: Factors influencing potential students' choices of doctoral programs in student affairs. *College Student Affairs Journal, 16*(1), 5–15.

Tinto, V. (1975) Dropout from Higher Education: A Theoretical Synthesis of Recent Research. *Review of Educational Research, 45*(1), 89–125.

Van Camp, D., Barden, J., Sloan, L. R., & Clarke, R. P. (2009). Choosing an HBCU: An opportunity to pursue racial self-development. *The Journal of Negro Education, 78*(4), 457–468.

Walker, R. (2008). *Buying in*. New York: Random House.

Weidman, J. C., Twale, D. J., & Stein, E. L. (2001). *Socialization of graduate and professional students in higher education: A perilous passage?* San Francisco: Jossey-Bass.

4 Graduate-Level Education at Historically Black Colleges and Universities
A Three-Part Qualitative Exposition

Antonio L. Ellis, Christopher N. Smith, and Janatus A. Barnett

Introduction: Exploring Counter-Narratives of Three Black Males

This chapter shares three counter-narratives. The first counter-narrative shares Ellis's experiences as Black man who received his primary education from predominantly Black schools and postsecondary education from Historically Black Colleges and Universities (HBCUs). However, while studying in K–12 schools and while completing his bachelor's degree from an HBCU, he was highly encouraged by Black teachers and professors not to attend an HBCU for graduate studies. They contended that people who received bachelor and graduate degrees from HBCUs are less likely to be as employable as persons who studied at predominantly White institutions (PWIs). Unfortunately, Ellis took the advice of these teachers and professors seriously. Therefore, after Ellis completed his undergraduate work, he remained committed to gaining admission into a PWI.

The second counter-narrative shares Smith's experiences as a Black male who received his primary education from predominately White schools and his postsecondary education from HBCUs. While completing his postsecondary education, he noticed a lack of respect toward his education from an HBCU, compared to his secondary school classmates who were attending PWIs. Additionally, when discussing his aspirations for graduate studies, he was confronted by more negative attitudes concerning HBCUs coupled with consistent pressure to seek admission into graduate programs at PWIs, from Blacks and non-Blacks alike. Smith struggled with the notion that HBCUs could not compare to PWIs even after attaining two degrees and found himself at a fork in the road when applying for doctoral programs.

The third counter-narrative shares Barnett's experiences as a Black male who received his primary education from the Baltimore City Public Schools. Thereafter he enrolled into Coppin State University for his undergraduate studies. After completing his undergraduate studies, Barnett returned to Coppin State for a portion of his graduate-level education. In order to diversify this chapter, he briefly shares his experiences as a student at Coppin State. Currently, Barnett is pursuing a master's degree at the University of Baltimore.

A Counter-Narrative by Antonio L. Ellis

K–12 Education: My Point of Departure

While receiving my primary education from the Charleston County Public Schools in the inner city of Charleston, South Carolina, my Black peers and I were constantly informed that we had to be as good as White children at schools located in the wealthier neighborhoods. Although the urban schools that we attended received hand-me-down books, computers, and appliances from the White schools, we were still expected to intellectually compete with them. As a Black male with a speech impediment, I constantly struggled internally to understand why Black students were treated differently than White students. However, because of my speech impediment, I did not feel physically capable or mentally empowered to verbally challenge institutionalized systems of inequality. Over the last fifty years, the general consensus has been that people with speech and language disorders are disadvantaged both socially and academically (Hartlep & Ellis, 2012; Logan, Mullins, & Jones, 2008). As a result of my feelings of powerlessness, I continued to marvel at the perceived lifestyle of Whiteness and secretly desired to obtain it. Charleston, South Carolina, is a city that is arguably rooted and grounded in Whiteness. The majority of the local key decision makers have traditionally been White. For example, Mayor Joseph P. Riley was elected as the mayor on December 15, 1975. He is currently serving his tenth term in office, making him one of the longest-serving mayors who is still living and in office. Therefore, throughout my K–12 schooling journey, I never saw diversity within the ranks of my local mayoral leadership.

From Howard University to Georgetown University

After graduating from Burke High School in Charleston, South Carolina, I attended Benedict College in Columbia, South Carolina. Benedict College has been one of the fastest growing of thirty-nine United Negro College Fund (UNCF) Schools. Of the twenty independent colleges in South Carolina, Benedict has the largest undergraduate student body and is the second largest overall. The college has students enrolled from every county in South Carolina. More than 3,200 students currently study at the school, and it is distinguished by its continued commitment to facilitate the empowerment, enhancement, and full participation of Blacks in a global society. While studying at Benedict College, not only did I develop academically, but I also developed a higher self-esteem, a deeper commitment to serving my community, and a passion for continual success throughout life. In 2004, I completed a bachelor of arts degree in religion and philosophy at the college. Because of the firm academic foundation that Benedict provided during my matriculation, I applied to graduate school at the Howard University School of Divinity. Howard University is a federally chartered, private, educational, nonsectarian, historically Black university located in Washington, DC. It has a Carnegie Classification of Institutions of Higher Education status of RU/H: Research Universities for high research activity.

While studying at Howard University, within the depths of my being, I felt as if my education was not good enough because I was attending graduate school at an HBCU. I mentally and emotionally held on to the advice that previous educators gave me regarding attending HBCUs for both my undergraduate and graduate studies. Regardless of being taught by leading theological and religious scholars at Howard, I still felt inadequate at the time. As a result of my feelings of inadequacy, during my final semester at Howard in 2006, I applied for admission to the Georgetown University School of Liberal Arts, where I pursued a graduate degree in liberal arts education. Established in 1789, Georgetown University in the nation's oldest Catholic and Jesuit university. The university website states "we provide students with a world-class learning experience focused on educating the whole person through exposure to different faiths, cultures and beliefs . . . Georgetown offers students a distinct opportunity to learn, experience and understand more about the world." According to the university website, as of fall 2013, the racial demographics were 48 percent White, 21 percent African American, 18 percent Asian, 9 percent Hispanic/Latino, and 4 percent other races. I finally obtained my goal of Whiteness.

Black, Male, and Speech Impaired at a Predominantly White Graduate Program

After being admitted into Georgetown University, I finally felt as if my education was meaningful and legitimate. During my first day on campus, with haste, I purchased university paraphernalia. After being accepted into a PWI, I also felt delighted to be accepted by the dominant culture (Whiteness). While attending classes with White students, I subconsciously noticed that both Benedict College and Howard University prepared me to be competitive at a PWI. As a result, during my first semester at Georgetown University, I didn't earn any grade less than a 3.0 on their 4.0 scale. Following a successful semester at Georgetown, I scheduled a meeting with the associate dean of the school of liberal arts. The purpose of this meeting was to inquire about merit-based scholarships and work-study opportunities that were offered by the department. On the day of the meeting, I arrived at the associate dean's office thirty minutes early so that she would view me as a punctual person. I was determined to maintain and increase my connections to Whiteness. Upon entering the associate dean's office, the administrative assistant greeted me and asked for my name and the time of my scheduled appointment. Due to my speech impediment, I experienced fluency challenges while trying to say my name and the time of my appointment. Thereafter, with some discomfort, I reached into my book bag for pen and paper and wrote the information that the administrative assistant requested.

Approximately thirty minutes later, the associate dean called me into her office. She closed her office door and proceeded to ask me to tell her about my experiences at Georgetown so far. Again, because of my stuttering disability, I experienced challenges verbally communicating. While I was struggling to communicate with her verbally, in a cruel tone of voice, she asked, "What's wrong with you?" At that point, I felt as if my approval by Whiteness started to dwindle. Therefore, with haste, I started to write a note to her explaining that I was speech impaired. While I was writing the note, she stormed out of the office for about five minutes. When she returned, I gave the note to her and nervously awaited for her response. After reading my note she said, "I will contact your professors. If you cannot get your words out, then Georgetown is not the university where you need to be. Perhaps you should consider applying to an online school. In order to be successful in our program, you must be able to speak aloud during classroom discussions."

At that point, I experienced multiple emotions and thoughts consecutively. My self-esteem plummeted, and my self-confidence was broken. Whereas I always had thoughts about what people authentically thought about my speech impediment, this was the first time someone blatantly discriminated against me because of it. Prior to leaving the associate dean's office, she said, "I am going to remove you from the program. Would you like advice for some online programs that would better accommodate your needs?" With my eyes filled with tears, I responded by writing, "No, ma'am, thank you for your time." While walking across campus for the final time as a student, I realized that my combination of being Black, male, and speech impaired made me a triple minority. Regardless of being admitted into Georgetown and earning competitive grades, I still was rejected by Whiteness.

Taking Another Look at Historically Black Colleges and Universities for Graduate Education

After the associate dean of the Georgetown University School of Liberal Arts removed me from the program in December 2006, I was forced to take a semester out of school because it was too late to apply to start any academic program in spring 2007. In addition, I needed time to mourn my disconnection to Whiteness and figure out which academic program I would apply to next. I wrestled with two questions. Should I apply for admission into another PWI? Should I apply for admission into another HBCU? During this time, I also started to spend a considerable amount of time thinking about ways to advocate on behalf of Black males who are speech and language impaired. My insensitive rejection from Whiteness triggered a passion in me to prevent my peers from experiencing the pain I experienced. Based on my reflections of my experiences at HBCUs and at Georgetown, I intentionally decided to return to Howard University to pursue a master's degree in educational administration and policy, with a special focus in special education. In light of being unethically rejected from a PWI by an educational administrator because of my disability, I developed a desire to become an educational leader to combat unjust racial and disability discrimination in K–12 and higher education institutions.

Social Justice–Driven Graduate Education

Upon my return to Howard University, I became more involved in my education than some of my colleagues who were pursuing graduate degrees in educational leadership only for career advancements. My return to study at Howard University was driven by a deeply rooted commitment to social justice. In addition, I returned to Howard with an appreciation for the nurture, acceptance, and care that I didn't receive from Georgetown University. During the 2008 spring semester, the Howard University department of educational administration and policy (now educational leadership and policy studies) received a US of Department of Education grant. As a result, the principal investigator of the grant and my professor, Dr. Saravanabhavan, invited me to attend the American Educational Research Association (AERA) Annual Meeting, which was held in Manhattan, New York. This was my first time attending an academic conference. I met a litany of educators and established great relationships with graduate students and junior faculty from national and international universities, including one of the editors of this book, Dr. Robert Palmer.

While at this national meeting with over five thousand registered, I noticed that less than 10 percent of the presenters were from HBCUs. In addition, over the four-day span of the meeting, I only met two people who graduated from an HBCU; however, they were teaching at PWIs. In the midst of conversations during the meeting, I informed faculty and graduate students that I was interested in becoming a professor after I earned a doctoral degree. My peers were only interested in teaching at PWIs. When I mentioned the possibilities of teaching at an HBCU, I received responses that reflected the advice I received about HBCUs before I was admitted into Georgetown University. The consensus was, "HBCUs don't pay enough; HBCUs don't have enough research funding; HBCUs are not research oriented; HBCUs are not respected academically; HBCUs aren't good enough." However, based on my experiences at a PWI, those negative comments regarding HBCUs increased my commitment to those institutions. The education I was receiving from Howard University was state of the art and second to none. My professors were competent practitioners and researchers, who graduated from leading schools such as Howard University, Harvard University, Yale

University, Morehouse College, Temple University, Duke University, Princeton University, Spelman College, University of Chicago, and the University of Illinois at Urbana-Champaign, among other nationally respected colleges and universities.

Misleading Assumptions About Historically Black Colleges and Universities

As stated in the previous section, there are several assumptions about HBCUs. However, based on my experiences at these prestigious institutions, these assumptions are misleading. This section will showcase a few successful HBCU graduates in order to serve as a counter-narrative against the ideology:

> Lonnie Rashid Lynn Jr. (also known as "Common") attended Florida A&M University, earning a degree in business administration before some recognition by *The Source* Magazine propelled his career into rap and acting.
> Toni Morrison is a Nobel Prize–winning author of such esteemed classics as *Song of Solomon* and *Beloved*. She graduated from Howard University with a degree in English in 1953.
> Gloria Ladson-Billings, PhD, is the Kellner Family Professor of Urban Education in the Department of Curriculum & Instruction at the University of Wisconsin-Madison and the 2005–2006 president of the American Educational Research Association. She graduated from Morgan State University in 1968.
> John Harkless, PhD, is an award-winning associate professor of chemistry at Howard University. He earned a bachelor of science degree in mathematics and chemistry from Morehouse College in 1995.
> Rev. Jessie Jackson, the civil rights activist often regarded as among the most important of Black leaders, graduated from North Carolina A&T University in 1964.
> Colbert L. King earned a government studies degree from Howard University. King used his writing prowess to earn a Pulitzer Prize during his tenure as a columnist for the *Washington Post*.
> Jerry Rice graduated from Mississippi Valley State University. He's not recognized as the greatest wide receiver in the NFL history but among the greatest at any position, winning three Super Bowls with the San Francisco 49ers, as well as an AFC Championship with the Oakland Raiders.
> Herman Cain, a successful businessman and 2012 republican presidential nominee, graduated from Morehouse College in 1967. He studied mathematics.
> Spike Lee graduated from Morehouse College in 1979, where he also lensed his first student film, *Last Hustle in Brooklyn*.

Thurgood Marshall, a graduate of Lincoln University, became the first African American Supreme Court Justice.

Wayne A.I. Frederick, MD, entered Howard University as a sixteen-year-old to pursue his dream of becoming a physician. He earned a dual BS/MD degree and went on to enter a surgical residency at Howard University. He was named one of America's Best Physicians by *Black Enterprise* magazine. Frederick currently serves at the seventeenth President of Howard University.

Deliberations of HBCU Success Stories

These selected success stories of HBCU graduates are counter to what I've been told about HBCUs over the past two decades. The Higher Education Act of 1965, as amended, defines an HBCU as: "any historically Black College or University that was established prior to 1964, whose principal mission was, and is, the education of Black Americans, and that is accredited by a nationally recognized accrediting agency or association" (Diamond, 2003). HBCUs offer all students, regardless of race, an opportunity to develop their skills and talents. These institutions train people who become domestic and international experts in various fields of study, as shown in the counter-narratives.

Embracing My Blackness

This section reveals my epistemological foundations as a Black male, who became comfortable with my Blackness after losing my appetite for Whiteness. I am reminded of my lived experiences in academic environments as a Black male who stutters, particularly my experience with the associate dean at Georgetown University. Now, as an emerging scholar in the field of education and as one who aims to lay a new foundation within the academy, I am challenged to revisit my epistemological commencement as a way to evaluate my sources of knowledge, my perspectives on the world, and more importantly, my beliefs about educational spaces for Black males who are speech and language impaired, particularly those who stutter.

Although I share a very similar background with this population of males, we endure different experiences due to our separate locations, support systems, parental involvement, safety nets, advocacy, and self-perceptions. In light of experiencing marginalization, discrimination, and arguably racism at Georgetown, I am propelled to embrace my Blackness, HBCUs, and speech and language impairment. As a child who avoided verbal communication because of my blackness combined with a stuttering disability, I navigated school buildings in urban communities in which I was raised in silence. As a Black male emerging scholar on who has received one of the highest academic degrees from an HBCU, I represent the potential brilliance embedded within my peers who are marginalized within White educational spaces. I was blessed to have had a high school band director, Mr. Linard McCloud (Burke High School), and pastors, Bishop Brian D. Moore (Life Center Ministries, Charleston, South Carolina) and Rev. Dr. Howard John-Wesley (Alfred Street Baptist Church, Alexandria, Virginia) who, in my early development and young adulthood, recognized my potential abilities and nurtured my dreams. Because of their involvement in my life, I have been able to supersede boundaries that many people set for me because of my stuttering disability. My high school band director demanded that I never give up in the face of adversity and what I perceived to be hopelessness. Therefore, I am motivated by a fierce sense of self-empowerment, a desire to empower others who are marginalized, a passion for educational achievement, and a sense of responsibility to mobilize those who are silenced and are unable to speak up for themselves.

My desire to advocate for marginalized groups of people has a sturdy religious and social justice base. My first advanced degree is in theological studies. I sought a theological degree hoping to gain a better understanding of my experiences as a stutterer. During my matriculation in divinity school, I gained a deeper understanding of my experiences by studying the writings of contemporary authors such as Cain Hope Felder, Dr. Martin Luther King Jr., Gregory Carr, Marcus Garvey, Reinhold Neihbuhr, W.E.B. Du Bois, and Fannie Lou Hamer. Regardless of their various perspectives, each of them dedicated and committed their lives to standing on behalf of minority groups who were marginalized by Whiteness. Therefore, my spiritual, religious, and theological base represents an extensive amount of social and Black Nationalist movements that were dedicated to altering racism, feminism, dominance, sexism, ageism, and White supremacy within the US context.

It is my belief that one of the most influential tools for providing positive change in the life of disenfranchised populations is education and the acquisition of knowledge. However, there is a large possibility that an educational structure embedded in fluency-dominated cultures, where the "gift of gab" is used to maintain social and economic power, can be seen as an advantage to White Supremacist. Regardless of race, those who are nonfluent often live in poverty and are positioned at the bottom due to the lack of reasonable accommodations, patience, and acceptance by those who are more fluent. However, being a Black male and speech impaired does not make this phenomena any better within a democratic society that is dominated by White power. Educators in urban environments rarely, if ever, highlight Black males who stutter and have excelled in various careers so that male students who stutter can gain inspiration. To teach a child, particularly a Black male who stutters, only the accomplishments and contributions of White non-stutterers creates a sense of doubt and hopelessness that he cannot achieve his goals in life. He will never be White, and his stuttering possibly may not be cured. Human beings tend to be motivated by what we can see, hear, taste, touch, and smell.

My greatest accomplishment thus far has been my presence in urban school buildings, higher education classrooms, and academic conferences. As an educator and advocate, I feel that it is my ministry, obligation, and duty to motivate students who live the same realities that I did as a child and into adulthood. My obligation is to assist them in developing strength and boldness to pursue their dreams in the face of multiple adversities. I have had the privilege and honor of meeting some of the most talented, intelligent, and bright minds who have been silenced by fear, just as I was prior to unhooking from Whiteness. These Black children possesses an undeniable glow that demands attention and validation, which I wholeheartedly gave. While spending time in school districts that are classified as urban, I constantly reflect on my own experiences and realities. It is because of the struggles of my students that I realized the significance of my own life history; therefore, I now embrace healing through advocating for my peers (children and adults) who face the same obstacles.

The personal relationships I developed with Black males who stutter via my work as a researcher, educator, and peer have been extremely rewarding. I have come to understand and embrace the significance of our lives and relationships. I was reared in communities that are somewhat identical to theirs, and I understand and identify with their struggles, concerns, pains, and cultural codes. Using my personal stories, experiences, and humor, I have worked diligently to relate to their everyday lives. In light of my upbringing as a student influenced by social and political movements like the civil rights movement and the Black Panther Party, I feel a fierce sense of urgency in eradicating systems of inequality, suppression, oppression, and White Supremacy. Therefore, my intellectual contribution to the field of education will also be to give support to the expansion of novel, innovative, and critical theoretical frameworks. West (1993) in his article, "The Dilemma of the Black Intellectual" refers to a new "regime of truth" that challenges scholars of color to analyze and critically examine the unique experiences of Black Americans, including those who are hooked to Whiteness.

I developed a deep commitment to transforming schools such that more Black Americans will graduate and become productive and respected citizens in society. Therefore, my research focuses specifically on revealing their stories and developing systems of support and offers possibilities that may work toward helping them to be successful in academic environments and in the larger society. An examination of these "possibilities for success" is meant to be a catalyst and prototype for disrupting educational institutional practices in regard to how Black students are included and/or not included. My goal is to deconstruct and challenge the status quo of educational spaces that have produced decades of negative stereotypes of Blacks, persons with disabilities, and HBCUs. Dillard (2000), Scheurich and Young (1997), and West (1993) all urge Black scholars to be bold enough to embrace their stance as Black Americans within the academy and to deliberately focus on the mobility of Black people if they desire to do so. In the midst of investigating and crafting educational scholarship that gives direct attention to Black students and debunking myths about HBCUs' graduate-level education, I hope that additional research paradigms and supportive peer-reviewed scholarship will emerge to interrogate Whitewashed opinions about our beloved institutions, while shedding light on the success stories of Black Americans and HBCUs.

Recommendations: Where Do HBCUs Go From Here?

Currently, few HBCUs offer graduate degrees in higher education. Therefore, these institutions are not represented among the producers of higher education administrators. Black Americans who want to pursue graduate degrees in higher education may be forced to attend PWIs because they have no option among HBCUs. While studying at Howard University, I was constantly told by my professor Dr. Lois-Harrison Jones, "If you are absent from the table, then you just may be a part of the menu." HBCUs are absent from the table in this regard; therefore, Black Americans are learning how to be higher education professionals from the perspective of Whiteness. At a recent educational leadership and policy meeting held at Howard University, Dr. Melanie Carter stated, "A graduate degree in higher education program at an HBCU would require designing a culturally based curriculum grounded in the theory and practice of higher education leadership and policy." It is imperative that HBCUs develop sustainable graduate degree programs in higher education that would produce culturally relevant leaders throughout the nation.

A Counter-Narrative by Christopher N. Smith

The greatest struggle in life has been to accept that skin tone does not equate to intellectual deficiency. As the son of a military officer and a stay-at-home mother, living in middle class society, benefiting from all the "privileges," it could be easily assumed that my life was easy. However, that assumption grossly misconstrues the harsh racial realities that existed and still exist within the context. While growing up I was faced with constant comparisons to my White classmates from kindergarten through high school. I was taught that to succeed I must be better than them in all areas. I was told that I must perform better academically, I must be more athletically skilled, and socially I could not reveal myself as too confident or I would be perceived as a threat. I was in a constant fight with identity, oscillating between the dominant White ideologies of self, the family expectations that were deeply rooted in Americanized Christianity, the popular Black culture that was burnt into my mind through media, and the uncultivated connection to an ancestry that I only heard about in part during Black History Month. These influences weighed heavy on my self-confidence and self-perception. At one point in time I even remember regretting being Black.

Howard University was when the narrative changed and always has been. At Howard is where I am consistently surrounded by people of color from all over the world just like me. I continue to come into contact with individuals and learned of people of color who were socially and intellectually striving to better themselves outside of the stereotypical "White" and "Black" cultural narratives that I have experienced. I continue to expand my knowledge about people of color worldwide, presently and historically, who have contributed to the human legacy. Enhancing my understanding of individuals like Kelly Miller, W.E.B. Du Bois, Stokley Carmichael, Huey P. Newton, Angela Davis, and the many who have impacted my doctoral field of study provides positive and progressive reference points. Reading about the history of Africa and other lands from the perspective of people of color continues to drastically alter my self-conception for the better. I felt so fulfilled with the first graduate experience that it led me to pursue my doctoral degree at Howard University as well.

However, when applying to doctoral programs, there was a bit of apprehension in only applying to Howard. I often struggled with deciding between attending Arizona State University and Howard University. Arizona State University has accumulated many accolades, and I truly felt that a degree from there would have given me a better chance at postgraduate employment. However, when I applied for their doctoral program, I was flatly rejected, and they offered instead to enroll me into their master's program. Arizona State felt I could "benefit" from the coursework offered and that I was not prepared enough for their program. That was a shock and a blow to the pride in my educational accomplishments I had earned. It was as if my education was subpar to them, like my hours of studying under some of the most accomplished and prolific scholars of color were inadequate.

However, it was in that moment that I realized my attendance at an HBCU for a doctorate was a necessity. I have a responsibility to myself and others like me to exemplify what an HBCU education can do. The PWI-advocating and HBCU-bashing ideology never settled well with me; actually I found it to be quite contradictory. If for eighteen years of my life I had been learning through the filter of Whiteness, would it not make sense that in order to be "well versed" I should spend the same amount of time learning from another filter? I found that attending HBCUs did exactly opposite of what I had been told. When I appear at conferences and interact with academic colleagues, I quickly come to understand how my education has made me more holistically aware in my field of study. Counter to popular belief, it is my HBCU education that has allowed me to have the opportunity to excel, work on multiple publications, and attend multiple conferences while earning a 4.0 GPA. In addition, the social justice focus of the doctoral program has prepared me to excel in internship opportunities with District of Columbia government agencies that advocate for previously incarcerated youth.

The depth and width of academic and personal growth that I've attained, I solely attribute to my education at HBCUs. PWIs and HBCUs alike have a lot to offer. However, if we as a human race are going to begin to see ourselves transcend racial stereotypes and racist inclinations, we too must began to challenge the manner in which we think about education. When people rely on surface appearances and false racial stereotypes, rather than in-depth knowledge of others at the level of the heart, mind, and spirit, their ability to assess and understand people accurately is compromised. This reliance must be altered so that educated people, no matter from where they matriculated, can began lauded for their accomplishments and afforded the opportunities they have worked to earn.

The Difficulties of HBCU Graduate Schools

Howard University since 1867 has attempted to be the "pillar of light" in education through truth and service. In its near 150-year lifespan, Howard University boasts of producing brilliant and influential minds worldwide that without question display a certain refined fever within every field of human endeavor. Unfortunately, Howard's legacy also includes incidents of fund misappropriation, resource mismanagement, and a slow evolution into technological advancements. The morning of September 4, 2015 a collection of students decided to exercise their right to organize by conducting a sit-in within the Modercai Johnson Administration Building to voice their grievances by covering facility pillars with post-its, listing the issues they had been facing. Instances like these are nothing new within the Howard University community. In the last ten years alone there have been multitudes of student demonstrations. However, some of the same operational and administrative issues still persist year after year. Proactive reformative thoughts and actions concerning education, technological trends, and funding opportunities are necessary for the continued advancement of HBCU graduate programs. It is not all the administration's responsibility, however. Students may have to take more responsibility in acquiring vital resources for the university's benefit and their own.

It was not until the early 2000s that Howard University began to attempt to provide quality Internet and online services. To this day, the use of technology that enhances learning experiences, such as smart boards and document cameras, are nearly nonexistent within the classrooms or nonoperational if provided. Many of the staff and faculty need access and training on the most recent advancements in educational and administrative technologies. Howard University does provide mind-altering and challenging rhetoric, such as it can't guarantee that your grades and financial aid are updated in the system, or that students can receive the funds they've worked diligently to earn. Pedagogical practices at HBCUs may also be problematic. Some have pointed out disconnections between the theoretical presentations that are meant to expand the students' awareness and instruction in how to practically put these theories and lessons into real life capital-accumulating solutions. As a student now aware of America's questionable history concerning race relations and the atrocities that people of African descent worldwide experience to this day, I always ask myself, "What can I do about it"? Students may not be able to acquire jobs or build new enterprises if they are not strategically trained to compete in the current market. Pushing students to be revolutionary and reformative elements also requires exposure to resources and tools, many of which HBCUs seems to lack.

Proposal writing for grants is a clear example of an underemphasized and rarely taught skill at HBCUs. It is clear that to progress, minority research institutions need to acquire this invaluable skill. However, mandatory grant-reading and proposal-writing courses within undergraduate and graduate curriculum are still not implemented at many HBCUs. Many professors do not attempt to acquire substantial grants, and neither has there been a vocalized push for grant acquisition and proposal writing as a requisite for continued professorship. Also, there have been few, if any, student collectives that have attempted to organize and write proposals on behalf of the university, or pressure the faculty that will not or have not.

Research at HBCUs support does bring in some resources; however, they do not tap into the wealth of opportunities that are now available within today's society. One example is the marijuana industry. The marijuana industry is an infant multibillion-dollar industry, although it is not fully legalized. Imagine if Howard University, which is located in a marijuana decriminalization area, began to tailor aspects of its business, sociology, political science, law, architecture, chemistry, medical, and biology programs toward producing policy and testing research that can provide pivotal components to the advancement of this industry. The possible resources and partnerships that the university could acquire would be astronomical. In addition, this may posture Howard graduates to become pioneers and influential figures within an international industry. Again, however, there hasn't been any student or faculty pressure on administration to consider programs and opportunities like these for Howard University or other HBCUs. To that end, students have not taken the initiative to collectively develop those programs and present them for administrative consideration and support. HBCU graduate education is a great experience. It can provide so many benefits and connections and facilitate innumerable personal and professional growth opportunities. However, to reach its maximal potential, it must maximize its capacity for change and adapt its programming to the fast-paced technology-oriented culture of the society surrounding it.

A Counter-Narrative by Janatus Barnett

HBCUs are very important institutions of higher learning for Black men and women. During my undergraduate and part of my graduate education, I had the privilege of attending one of the best HBCUs in the nation, Coppin State

University (CSU) of Baltimore, Maryland. The professors were great, and the milieu for learning was unlike anything I have ever experienced. The professors at Coppin knew my name, and they never made me feel like I was just another student ID number. I grew up in Baltimore, where, in my opinion, the public schools were overcrowded and not conducive for a healthy learning environment. Upon entering Coppin State as an undergraduate student, I immediately gained an appreciation for the low student-to-teacher ratio. Similarly, I noticed even smaller classroom sizes in Coppin State's graduate program.

Coppin State University is an HBCU that truly nurtures its students. The support I received from my professors made me want to excel in academia and in life. The faculty knew how to maximize my potential by teaching me the effectiveness of critical thinking. Before I enrolled into Coppin State University, I never questioned things I understood to be societal norms. However, after studying at Coppin State, I departed with a progressive outlook on life. Historically, HBCUs are known to be more culturally diverse than other universities. I recommend HBCU graduate programs to anyone who appreciates diverse cultural experiences. I am currently at student at the University of Baltimore, which is a PWI; nevertheless, I believe it was my experience at Coppin State that allowed me to appreciate diversity among all cultures.

While at Coppin State, I was privileged to meet people and build networks with international colleagues. These international networks included people from Africa, Canada, China, Haiti, and Jamaica, among other countries. Although other graduate schools offer similar experiences, I believe that my experience at Coppin State was unique and tailor made to accommodate my needs as a student. Unlike some universities, whose priority is to improve retention rates, Coppin State focuses on student learning. Students with different facets of life were given a platform to be heard and valued. I believe Coppin's rudimentary approach to teaching can be helpful for all HBCUs. Coppin promoted an environment that embraced the individuality of each student.

Most universities welcome students from diverse backgrounds and cultures; however, they do not provide outlets for students to express their various cultures. There is an old expression, "There's some things that money can't buy." Money could never buy the experience I had at Coppin State University. The costs to attend graduate school at a PWI is significantly more expensive than to attend an HBCU. Fortunately, this was not an issue for me because I am a veteran and was able to use my post-9/11 GI Bill education benefit to help fund my graduate education. Whereas I had the opportunity to attend other colleges and universities, I chose Coppin State for both my undergraduate and a portion of my graduate-level studies. I believe students should attend HBCUs in their hometown, if applicable. Coppin State University is a school of study for the liberal arts. Dr. W. E. B Du Bois is well known for his positionality on the importance of a liberal arts education.

He believed students should be well versed in many things and share what they've learned with others in their communities. Whereas I can only share my personal experiences at Coppin State, I believe students who attend HBCUs are more compelled to invest in their communities. Coppin State University prepared me to be a leader in my community. Attending an HBCU for both undergraduate and graduate studies was one of my best decisions.

Conclusion

This chapter is not intended to promote HBCUs or to speak negatively of PWIs; however, the authors intended to debunk and resist dominant notions that HBCUs are less-credible academic institutions. HBCUs offer culture, a rich history, and rigorous academic programs. Most importantly, they prepare students for leadership and life beyond graduation. Whereas HBCUs represent only 3 percent of the nation's institutions of higher education, they graduate nearly 20 percent of Blacks who earn undergraduate degrees (Perna, 2001). In addition, these institutions graduate more than 50 percent of Black professionals and public school teachers (Brown & Davis, 2001). HBCUs hold a unique legacy to the specific needs of young Black minds and continue to demonstrate the most effective ability to graduate Black students poised to be competitive in the corporate, research, academic, governmental, and military arenas. The authors urge all HBCU scholars to unhook from Whiteness by publicly defending the worth, value, and importance of our institutions. Lived experiences must continuously be shared in order to explicate White ideology and unlock possibilities for challenging their hegemony, just as auto-ethnographic stories by and about people from oppressed communities offer strategies for challenging domination. Challenging dominant notions is not popular or convenient; however, it is necessary for the preservation of our communities and educational institutions.

References

Brown, M. C., & Davis, J. E. (2001). The historically Black college as social contract, social capital, and social equalizer. *Peabody Journal of Education, 76*(1), 31–49. doi: 10.1207/S15327930PJE7601_03

Diamond, A. A. S. (2004). Serving the educational interests of African-American students at Brown plus fifty: The historically Black college or university and affirmative action programs. *Tulane Law Review, 78*, 1877.

Dillard, C. B. (2000). The substance of things hoped for, the evidence of things not seen: Examining an endarkened feminist epistemology in educational research and leadership. *International Journal of Qualitative Studies in Education, 13*(6), 661–681. doi: 10.1080/09518390050211565

Hartlep, N. D., & Ellis, A. L. (2012). Rethinking speech and language impairments within fluency-dominated cultures. In S. Pinder (Ed.), *American multicultural studies: Diversity of race, ethnicity, gender and sexuality* (pp. 410–430). Thousand Oaks, CA: Sage.

Logan, K. J., Mullins, M. S., & Jones, K. M. (2008). The depiction of stuttering in contemporary juvenile fiction. *Communication Disorders, 45*(7), 609–626. doi: 10.1002/pits.20313

Perna, L. W. (2001). The contribution of historically Black colleges and universities to the preparation of African Americans for faculty careers. *Research in Higher Education, 42*(3), 267–294. doi: 10.1023/A:1018869922415

Scheurich, J., & Young, M. (1997). Coloring epistemologies: Are our research epistemologies racially biased? *Educational Researcher, 26*(4), 4–16.

West, C. (1993). The dilemma of the Black intellectual. *The Journal of Blacks in Higher Education, 2*, 59–67.

5   Back to the Roots

Sheree Alexander

In 1990 when I graduated from high school, I was seventeen years old and had not seen a live cow. I knew cows came in black and white and brown and white. However, identifying what the jet black animal was standing along the road as I trekked up to Lancaster County to begin my freshman year at Millersville University did not come so easily. There are no cows in the Philadelphia zoo, and traveling through the miles and miles of farmland along Route 30 was like visiting a new world. I did not come through the Program for the Advancement of Compensentory Education (PACE), which was a summer program for students who may have needed to develop their basic skills before experiencing college-level courses, where many other students from neighborhoods like and unlike mine made their first lasting relationships. I started my undergraduate experience at Millersville University, most times the only Black student in all five of my classes. I was one of maybe three other students of color in courses. I often thought to myself, *Where is everyone else who looks like me? Where will the Black teachers come from?*

Black Educators—Where Have They Gone?

Whereas the *Brown v. Board of Education* 1954 decision is deemed by many to be the most significant event of the twentieth century that reduced both segregation and discrimination and opened the doors of opportunity for Black Americans, there are others who are equally concerned with whether Black students, in general, have materially benefited during the last fifty years, particularly given today's teacher and student demographics. Many scholars have lamented the fact that the vast majority of Black students have a sharply declining number of Black teachers to serve as role models for them (Lyons & Chesley, 2004). King (1993) contends that in addition to serving as positive role models for students, Black teachers also tend to serve as surrogate parents, disciplinarians, counselors, and advocates for Black students. The significance of discussing Black educators is due to the severe discrepancy between the teaching population and the student population within the United States.

There are several historical, political, economic, demographic, and sociological factors that have contributed to the decline in Black educators. Historically, teaching attracted a disproportionate number of poor and minority persons who looked to the profession as a means of upward mobility. This is especially true for Black females who were college graduates. Teaching in addition to social work and nursing was considered a prestigious job and one of the few career opportunities for Blacks (Irvine, 2002). The Supreme Court's ruling on *Brown v. Board of Education* created anticipation in Black educators who thought that the ruling would finally garner equal and better treatment for Black students and teachers.

Prior to desegregation, Black educators were teaching Black students. However, the 1954 decision changed everything and negatively impacted Black educators and Black students. One of the most damaging effects was the dismissal and demotion of Black principals and teachers. In 1954 when the decision was handed down, there were 82,000 Black teachers, and by 1964, 38,000 Black teachers and administrators had lost their positions (Lyons & Chesley, 2004). Prior to desegregation, Black schools that were semiautonomous were ignored by White administrators, but the 1954 Brown decision dictated that White school boards and superintendents were now in control of critical personnel decisions, such as hiring, firing, and transfers, in previously all-Black schools. Personnel decisions resulted in the firing and transferring of many Black teachers after desegregation became taken over and controlled by White administrators, and due to the lack of tenure and reduction in force policies being in place in those states most affected by the mandate to desegregate, Black teachers and administrators had little recourse to contest displacements or dismissals (Irvine, 2002; Lyons & Chesley, 2004).

Ethridge (1979) estimated that between 1954 and 1972 there were at least 39,386 documented cases of Black teachers losing their jobs in seventeen southern states. These numbers do not reflect the vast numbers of the Black community's most competent teachers, who were reassigned to schools in the White community, a prevalent practice then and now as some Black parents elected to send their children to formerly all-White schools. Whereas the majority of school board members and superintendents in states most affected were White, preferences were likely given to retaining and employing White principals and teachers. Racism continued to have a role in how decisions were made and implemented (Lyons & Chesley, 2004). Holmes (1990) points out that a cycle developed between 1960 and 1990 in which fewer students of color have been taught by teachers of color. There are many students of color matriculating through elementary and high school while having few, if any, Black teachers. The teaching profession in the United States has become increasingly White, whereas the student population has become increasingly minority and diverse (Lyons & Chesley, 2004).

Irvine (2002) has identified four factors that have contributed to the decreasing number of minority, specifically Black, teachers, which are: (1) the decline in the number of college students declaring teacher education majors; (2) the decline in Black college students; (3) widening career options for Blacks, especially Black females; and (4) the institutionalization of teacher competency tests. Irvine further posits that college attendance rates among Blacks in general are plummeting. King (1993) points out that between the early 1970s and the mid-1980s, the supply of new teachers fell substantially. Whereas education was once the most frequently chosen degree field for people of color, it had slipped to third, after business and the social sciences (ACE, 1988). The number of bachelor's degrees in education earned by Euro-American students decreased by 50 percent between 1975 and 1985, whereas the number of bachelor's degrees in education earned by Black students declined by 66 percent (Darling-Hammond, 1990). It is important to emphasize that the number of education degrees awarded to Black students severely declined disproportionately between 1976 and 1987 at both the bachelor's and the master's degree levels (King, 1993).

The Predominantly White Institution (PWI)

For one of the Intro to Urban Education courses, Ms. Kramer, our instructor who also happened to be a former Girls' High student, asked us to share something interesting about ourselves. Many of the students mentioned interesting things, so I shared with the entire class my discovery of the black cow. I thought it was interesting because even before I took one education course, I was thinking about what was considered as knowledge. Why couldn't I identify the black cow? Once the confession carried by my voice left my lips and sat suspended in the air surrounding this group of soon-to-be teachers, I regretted sharing anything personal or interesting about myself. My classmates were not laughing with me but were laughing at me. These young, middle-class White females, who were from various suburban or rural areas all across western Pennsylvania, found it hilarious that the only inner city Black girl in their class had not seen a live cow before. I will never forget the smug, incredulous looks on their faces, the dismissive flipping of their blond or brown hair as I sank as far into the small seat as I could.

That day, I unplugged, disconnected, and withdrew from the learning community. However, I showed up every day, counting the minutes of each class, wondering how the future brown, Black, and poor students, who would sit in similar seats in front of these same young women and others just like them, who would soon become part of the teaching force, would feel when they did the same thing to them. Already, I felt sad for children, many whom were not even born yet. Sad that they too just might experience the premature dimming of their inner light. This was one of the experiences that influenced my decision to attend an HBCU. I wanted, longed for the "other-mothering" I received in middle school. There is where I felt supported by the home-school community that was strong and evident in our "urban" community. There is also where I was identified as "at-risk," whatever that meant in 1986. After the fact, I appreciate the camaraderie of attending an all-girls' high school in the inner city. This competitive, admittance-based, college preparatory high school housed girls of many races, nationalities, and religions. We were empowered, inspired, and expected to be great girls and become greater women collectively. Yet, being female was not my only identity. What about the Black little girl? The little girl of a Black single mother? What about the young person who was all three, Black, poor, and female? Present yet invisible at the same time. This is another experience that influenced my decision to attend an HBCU. These experiences and the yearning for a deeper connection to myself influenced my decision to attend an HBCU. I wanted to learn more, research more, discover more in an inclusive environment where some things were just understood.

I did fairly well as an undergraduate at a PWI. I did not do as well as I could have for many reasons, but I persisted. I cannot identify a particular thing that enabled me to persist. It was more a set of things inclusive of but not limited to: being the first person in my family to graduate from college, beating the odds set for one raised by a single Black mother, and the need to meet and exceed the high expectations that my immediate family and caregivers had for me. Partly, if not mainly, I knew very early that if I, a Black girl from North Philadelphia, Pennsylvania, could get through the required four years in the farming Amish community of Lancaster County, I could do so much more for children who were just like me in so many ways.

I learned, as students have to, how to navigate a place that did not deny me entry but did not have me in mind when creating the climate and culture of the learning community. Where would I find professors who looked like me? In my discipline? On campus? Where were the coursework offerings that would enlighten me about the historical or current trends in education? What class could I take that would give me any indication of what being a Black teacher would be like? And more importantly, where were they? Where on campus would I find personal or hair care products that I needed? Socially, where did I go? Although I did not know it then, I questioned the true success rate of assimilation. Could everyone just do that, assimilate? I was there among thousands of other students doing what they did, going where they went, pretending that all was well in the world. I received a solid, well-rounded education that I value. I graduated with a degree and a desire to get to, as fast as I could, kids like me who would sit in front of me in my classroom and get what they were missing, something for them.

Culture

Culture is a variable that is often overlooked as a function of student success. The culture of schools often mirrors the White middle-class norms and values evident in the greater US society. This mismatch between school culture and the culture of students creates the potential for misunderstanding actions and misinterpreting communication between teacher and student

(Ware, 2006). Some ethnic minority students are negatively situated by the structure of schools, the mixed messages from peer social networks, and the many stresses that racism, cultural stereotypes, and poverty pose. This negative positioning can lead some to perceive tensions between their identities as members of a community and what they view as the demands of school (Lee, 2003).

Inner-city youth face numerous problems that are endemic to poor urban areas and that have the potential to interfere with these students' ability to learn and succeed in schools (Bemak, 2002; Bemak & Chung, 2003; Dryfoos, 1994, 1998; Jagers & Mock, 1993; Witherspoon, Speight, & Thomas, 1997). Noguera (2003) brings attention to the fact that poor children generally receive inferior services from schools and agencies that are located in the inner city, and poor children often have many unmet basic needs. As a field, education has moved away from certain classifications, only to move toward current terminologies (e.g., inner-city, at-risk) that carry with them similar sets of assumptions that continue to place groups in hegemonic opposition. Although most children living in poverty are classified as White, the terms "inner city" and "at-risk" remain code words for those who are not racially classified as White. Culture, then, becomes something we need to understand about the "other folks" (those who are not identified as White) (Lee, 2003).

Swanson, Cunningham, and Spencer (2003) state that there is still evidence of structural racism in American society, and it stems from systematic and institutionalized practices resulting in the subordination and devaluation of minority groups. The consequences of the process of subordination and devaluation for minority youth are twofold. First, minority youth growing and developing in late twentieth- and early twenty-first-century America often live and mature in high-risk environments, characterized by systemic, structural barriers to individual effort and success.

Second, instances of resilience, success, and competence displayed by minority youth in spite of adverse living conditions often go unnoticed and unrecognized, denying individuals a sense of success and accomplishment. Black youth become marginalized by the problems associated with their identity. Much of the research aligns with the notion that by the onset of adolescence, Black and other minority youth have developed an awareness of White American values and standards of competence (Spencer, Swanson, & Cunningham, 1991). They begin to integrate their experiences with future expectations given their own and their family's values, and those of the majority culture. Who, then, was I? I wanted, needed to know.

Back Home

I began my teaching career in Cleveland, Ohio, at Patrick Henry Middle School with a 98 percent African American student population. After that first year and an extremely cold and snowy winter, I was laid off and returned to the East Coast to have the honor and pleasure of teaching at the middle school, E. W. Rhodes, I attended as a student. I was elated to be back home teaching in the very classrooms I sat in as a student. I was even more excited about teaching with some of my former teachers. I was super excited about the opportunity to provide a safe and nurturing learning environment for children in my community, the community where I was born, raised, and still considered as "home." I looked forward to teaching the children and grandchildren of my neighbors. I had witnessed, firsthand, the deterioration of our community through the late '80s and early '90s. Drugs, poverty, and economics ate mercilessly at the familial bonds that neighbors had. These issues seeped into every nook and cranny of the community, including local businesses and most importantly but unfortunately, our schools. My excitement at returning to my former middle school was not diminished at first by the peeling paint, dark hallways, and almost apathy that came from the building principal. I went to this school! The reports of lagging performance, failing test scores, and dismal outlook made me even more determined to do something for the kids whose lives actually depended on what they would be able to take from their short years at E.W. Rhodes.

African American students face unique challenges in public education. The long-range, detrimental effects that stereotyping places on minority groups is underestimated (Sigelman & Tuch, 1997). This, along with some flawed teacher expectations that influence the performance of students, in turn sheds light on the notion that the Black-White achievement gap may in part result from the differential treatment that Black students receive in school (Ferguson, 1998). There is considerable evidence that the ethnic and socioeconomic backgrounds of students have a bearing on how students are perceived and treated by the adults who work with them within schools (Brookover & Erickson, 1969; Morrow & Torres, 1995). In contrast to the increased diversity of students, the population of teachers is becoming more homogeneous; that is to say, with each passing year there are fewer teachers of color to represent the diverse group of students in today's schools (Cooper, 2003; Futrell, 1999; Su, 1996). In fact, just over 10 percent of teachers come from racially or ethnically diverse groups (Eubanks, 1996). College graduates entering the teaching force, regardless of race or ethnicity, are not sufficiently prepared to teach ethnically diverse students (Gay, 2002). Many novice and veteran teachers lack the cultural awareness necessary to reach the diverse population of K–12 students, which results in further perpetuating the hegemonic culture that exists throughout American school.

Cultural Responsiveness

"Any educational or training system that ignores the history or perspective of its learners or does not attempt to adjust its teaching practices to benefit all its learners is contributing to inequality of opportunity" (Wlodkowski & Ginsberg, 1995, as cited by Brown, 2004, p. 267). In many schools across the United States, the teaching population does not reflect the student population, racially or culturally. This can cause a disconnect between teachers and students, ultimately depriving students of a quality education. There are missed cues and signals that can cause the learning process to become stagnant. Thus, educators exiting teacher preparation programs, leaving institutions of higher education, need to be prepared to implement methodology and techniques that are culturally responsive, in addition to being pedagogically sound. In essence, there needs to be a more diverse population of teachers in the field, so that the teaching population reflects more accurately the population of the student body.

Teaching that is not culturally responsive contributes to this trend. The structure and culture of schools play a major role in reinforcing and maintaining racial categories and the stereotypes associated with them. As schools sort children by perceived measures of their ability, and as they single out certain children for discipline, implicit and explicit messages about racial and gender identities are conveyed (Noguera, 2003). Explanations of the achievement gap relating to how schools are organized have concentrated on curriculum issues, teaching strategies, school achievement climate, and expectations. How schools structure students' opportunities to learn has been shown to influence academic achievement. If students do not believe that their teachers care about them and are actively concerned about their academic performance, the likelihood that they will succeed is greatly reduced (Noguera). This applies to the K–12 or higher education student.

Culturally responsive teaching involves responsive management, a caring attitude, establishing assertiveness and authority, and congruent communication processes while demanding effort. Culturally responsive management focuses on many teaching components and essential research-based pedagogical processes as well as the ability to respond appropriately to the emotional, social, ethnic, cultural, and cognitive needs of students. This is a complex process that involves interpersonal and pedagogical awareness and application in both realms (Brown, 2004).

Siddle-Walker (1996) noted that the attributes of Black teachers have a cultural history. In segregated schools, Black teachers typically emphasized the importance of education for political and economic success. The teachers were also united in their approach to developing students' awareness of the role of education in their lives. Black teachers have fulfilled many roles in the lives of Black students. Research conducted by Meier, Stewart, and England (1989) has also shown that the higher the percentage of Black teachers in schools, the lower the numbers of Black students placed in special education, or subjected to expulsion or suspension.

Brown (2004) believes that creating a positive learning environment requires attentiveness to the way in which teachers communicate with students. Culturally responsive teaching involves building relationships with students and displaying caring bonds and attitudes toward students as well as establishing community and family-type classroom environments, similar to Freire's (1970) revolutionary pedagogy, which started from a deep love for, and humility before, poor and oppressed people with respect for their "common sense," constituting a knowledge no less important than the scientific knowledge of the professional. Appreciating and accepting students' way of knowing opens doors for opportunity and equity (Collins, 1990).

The HBCU—Choosing Cheyney

The plight of the K–12 student, the undergraduate, and the postgraduate is common across all levels. The presence Black teachers and professors can give students an unspoken level of sense of comfort. I had earned a bachelor's degree in elementary education from a PWI. I had foundational grounding but not the historical grounding that affected Black students. Leading a classroom for a few years, I already realized the students who looked like me felt comfortable with me, the same way I felt comfortable with them. At the end of my fourth year of teaching, I decided to pursue a master's degree. I was teaching in the eighth-largest school district in the country and in the city I was born and raised in, the City of Brotherly Love, Philadelphia, Pennsylvania. While I was deciding which program to apply to, Cheyney University had implemented a program in which you could study within your own context, meaning the professors would come to a school and teach the introductory courses there. Not only was it convenient, but it made learning, for me, in real time. I could dismiss my students and go literally across the hall to class.

At the informational session, I had the opportunity to meet the professors for the four beginning courses. They all looked like me. They had all been former teachers and school administrators. During the informational session, I knew before it ended that I would be choosing to attend this HBCU in hopes of learning who I really was and how to better serve my students. I found the opportunity to attend and pursue my master's degree from Cheyney University an excellent opportunity to develop my leadership skills, which would enable me to be better equipped to address the quality of educational systems underserving Black children, engage our communities once again, and challenge the social justice issues that impact public schooling and prayerfully to lead a school where students are educated and nurtured holistically.

> *Only the BLACK WOMAN can say "when and where I enter, in the quiet, undisputed dignity of my womanhood, without violence and without suing or special patronage, then and there the whole . . . race enters with me."*
> —Anna Julia Cooper, 1892

The lens of intersectionality, which addresses race, class, and gender as intertwined factors that might alter the experience and meaning of each, best illuminates the often contradictory experiences of educational inequality for Black girls (Morris, 2007). Many of the early experiences in my life have played an integral part in shaping my leadership that is grounded in Black feminist theory (Cannon, 1988; Collins, 1991; Hooks, 2000), critical race theory (Bell, 1980; Crenshaw, 1988; Delgado & Stefancic, 1997; Ladson-Billings & Tate, 1995; Wing, 2000), and social justice theory (Cambron-McCabe & McCarthy, 2005; Giddings, 1984; Murtadha & Watts, 2005; Theoharis, 2005). My experiences as a Black female are unique and anchor my commitment to progressive change through a social justice paradigm for those who experience oppression at home, at work, in their communities, and moreover, within the dominant culture as a whole (Barnes, 2008).

I am aware that my past experiences greatly influence my approach to social justice leadership and the paradigms utilized in the quest for my truth. Social justice is informed by multidisciplinary inquiry that struggles to accommodate distinct ontological and epistemological foundations (Cambron-McCabe & McCarthy, 2005). Yet today's leadership models, although they may differ from person to person, and method to method, generally have a common bias toward Western- or European-influenced ways of thinking and approaches (Bordas, 2007), leaving many voices and perspectives unexplored. It is equally important, however, that others are aware that my leadership development has been a continuous process of change and reaction to life events that have occurred over time, as discussed by Conger and Kanungo (1988).

The past experiences and struggles of Black women who came before me have also shaped my leadership development. It would be difficult to accurately address my leadership development without taking into account the existential situation of Black women, which cannot be understood or explained adequately apart from this historical background (Cannon, 1988). Doing so has allowed me yet another lens through which to view my experiences and brings clarity to why my experiences and those of other Black women who aspire to be effective leaders in our communities and in society require specific attention. For this reason, I felt it was necessary for me to attend an HBCU where the social capital that I had acquired would be useful and helpful to me in ways that did not require me to simply comply, assimilate, and normalize the institutionalized oppression that was permeating the institution of education

Historically Black Colleges and Universities (HBCUs)

Whereas desegregation impacted K–12 education, higher education was impacted as well. One of the historical factors that has impacted the limited role of African American teachers is the role of HBCUs. Coaxum (2001) points out that whereas the research available on HBCUs is scant and not inclusive of the diversity that exists among and between HBCUs, there are research scholars who have continued to point out their importance, and the assets they provide for Black students that are unavailable to them at PWIs. These assets include offering an accepting environment, unconditional emotional support, and the environment conducive to fostering healthy social relationships. Whereas Coaxum (2001) points out the unique role that HBCUs have played in educating Black college students, he further posits that in order to fully understand the role that HBCUs have and continue to play in the education of African American students, they should be classified by variables unique to HBCUs and not just traditional classification variables. Whereas there is a noted decrease in attendance at HBCUs, scholars have pointed out that HBCUs educate students with learning deficiencies and provide opportunities for students to assume leadership roles, and from an academic perspective, scholars reported that Black students attending HBCUs perform better academically and also tend to go on to graduate school in higher proportions than do Black students attending PWIs (Allen, Epp, & Haniff, 1991).

Prior to 1945, HBCUs enrolled 90 percent of all Black students seeking postsecondary degrees (Garibaldi, 1991); prior to 1954, the majority of Black college students were enrolled in HBCUs; and by 1973, that percentage had plummeted to one-fourth (King, 1993). Collectively, between 1976 and 1989, there was a decrease in the percentage of degrees conferred by HBCUs, which also mirrors the decline in educational degrees across the board (King, 1993). This decline could be attributed to the opening up of more lucrative, prestigious career opportunities for Black students, other individuals of color, and women, which then questions the role of HBCUs (Dilworth, 1984) concerning their centrality and necessity.

King (1993) points out that the continuing legacy of racism in this country has manifested itself in federal and state financing guidelines and school certification requirements that have at times served to limit funding to HBCUs. This has, in turn, influenced HBCUs' abilities to prepare Black teachers (King, 1993), although these institutions graduate a higher proportion of Black students and have granted a disproportionate number of degrees to Blacks than any other segment of higher education (Coaxum, 2001). Yet, in a study conducted by Goldhaber, Perry, and Anthony (2004) on National Board for Professional Teaching Standards (NBPTS) certification, teachers who are Black, female, score higher on standardized tests, and/or are younger are more likely to apply for certification whereas the findings revealed that Black and male teachers are less likely to be certified, and teachers who score higher on standardized tests are far more likely to be certified. The conclusion of the study revealed a striking discrepancy in application and certification rates for Black teachers and applicants from disadvantaged schools.

In addition to the disparity in national teacher certification, Garibaldi's (1991) study explained the decline in the number of education degrees awarded by HBCUs and also indicated that only small numbers of Black, Louisianan education majors were able to become licensed after completing education degree programs due to their inability to achieve the passing NTE score.

Overall, my experience at Cheyney University pursuing a master's degree was positive. What I found to be most significant and comforting to me was the Black faculty. Most of our professors and instructors held terminal degrees in their field and had been or currently were practitioners as teachers, principals, and district superintendents. So, when there was a position presented in class, the conversation came from both a point of reference, personal and professional experience, in addition to contextual identification with the problem and the sought-after solution. I received valuable and genuine feedback on my assignments and projects. All of us in the cohort were afforded opportunities to discuss our classroom's or individual school's issues in confidence and with discretion without the threat of the opinions and comments made in class getting back to building staff, students, or administrators. I felt the difference in speaking with my professors about my questions and concerns. My responses were not generic, contrived, or required to be scheduled during office hours, which were of course during the hours I was working. So, I did not have to choose between addressing my questions and concerns or taking a sick day away from my classroom. Although this is what we do to parents when we schedule parent-teacher conferences during the school day when many work and are unable to attend during the scheduled times or have to possibly miss wages when they choose to come between 1:00 p.m. and 3:00 p.m. because teachers can and many will contractually leave even if the parent may be able to get to the school by 3:30 p.m. But I digress here for now.

Attending Cheyney University had a huge impact upon my choice to pursue school leadership. The most valuable part of choosing Cheyney's master's program was the contextual experience. My instructors were sharing research they had read or heard about, and they offered real, lived experiences as participant researchers even if they did not consider themselves as such while they held principalships, assistant superintendencies, and district supervisory positions. Through the Cheyney experience, I learned how to approach and solve existing problems in urban public schooling situations. In hindsight and retrospect, I learned how to delve a little deeper while proving sound instruction for my students. I learned too that many of the problems we were taught to approach, explore, address, and solve were most often one-dimensional. What I take from my experience at Cheyney University is the birth of my quest to fight for social justice for the underserved, marginalized, underfunded, and misunderstood students who come to school with all that they have and all of who they are wanting something more.

Challenges of Attending an HBCU

I had solid concerns about choosing to attend an HBCU to pursue a postgraduate degree. However, I was not deterred from attending Cheyney because although I, as a Black woman, could gain entry into a PWI, HBCUs were and had to be established because at one point Black students were neither welcomed not admitted to PWIs. Jones (2013) perfectly points out that nearly two hundred years into their existence, questions persist regarding the reputational worth of Historically Black Colleges and Universities.

Matriculation through Cheyney was not without any issues. The fiscal management had often been in question, and at one point Cheyney's accreditation was even threatened. Whereas *Brown vs. Board of Education* of 1954 is often referenced as the beginning point of discussion when discussing separate versus equal and desegregation in K–12, there were implications for higher education as well. Although unintentional, the *Morrill Act of 1890* cemented the prevailing doctrine of segregation. It formalized the manifestation of separate but unequal in higher education. The patterns of underfunding persist even today. Research data indicate that faculty salaries at HBCUs remain lower than those at PWIs. Furthermore, expenditures at public HBCUs are lower than those at other public institutions. Despite increases in enrollments across public and private HBCUs, they continue to be disproportionately worse off fiscally (Brown, 2013).

Anyone considering attending an HBCU for their graduate education should consider the following:

> One of the functions of HBCUs is to be repositories of Diaspora history and the history of social hostility. Although it is possible for African American students to attend any institution without prohibition based on race, this legal access to the institution does not guarantee authentic participation to the informal social networks within the institution. In fact, the college-going experiences of African American students on predominantly white campuses remain fraught with social isolation and cultural estrangement. HBCUs, on the other hand, have historically assumed a greater responsibility for educating African American students (Gurin & Epps, 1975) for participation in a broader society that has been exclusive, indifferent, and hostile. Also, HBCUs continue to provide the experience for African American students to become beneficiaries of their unique social capital. This ability is endemic to the functions of providing academic remediation, environmental support, and cultural relevance that appear to minimize the effects of differential precollege preparation. The transferal of the social information, achievement, and credentials needed for African Americans to enjoy full participation in the larger society remain a primary role of the Black college. This purveyance of social capital sustains the equalization of African Americans in the nation and world. Indeed, Black colleges are important mediators in the pursuit of African Americans for both equality of opportunity and equity in outcomes.
>
> (Brown & Davis, 2001, p. 15)

The quest of pursuing higher education is an individual decision that will be based upon many variables, such as your personal and professional circumstances and resources, your preference for on-line or brick and mortar, and your field of study. What I would suggest anyone consider is the process and experiences that will be generated during that experience. You will interact with other students with various backgrounds and undergraduate experiences. The nuances that exist in higher education will persist, but according to what you have identified as one of your personal needs versus your wants from a postgraduate program, your choice to attend an HBCU will be a very important one. For me, I attended a PWI as an undergraduate and personally did not have some of the supports, cultural connectedness, social capital, other mothering, or culturally responsive teaching that I needed as an undergraduate student. Therefore, my choice to attend an HBCU for my master's degree filled in many gaps, impacted my identity development, and allowed me to make realizations in a space that I considered as safe while matriculating.

References

Allen, W. R., Epp, E. G., & Haniff, N. Z. (1991). *College in Black and White: African American students in predominantly White and historically Black public colleges and universities*. Albany: State University of New York Press.

American Council on Education. (1988). Minorities in higher education: Sixth Annual Status Report. Washington, D.C.

Barnes, L. P. (2008). *Philosophy of Education Society of Great Britain: Religious education as if respect for persons and social cohesion really matters*. London: Impact Series.

Bell, D. (1980). *Shades of brown: New perspectives on school desegregation*. New York: Teachers College Press.

Bemak, F. (2002). Paradigms for future counseling programs. In C. D. Johnson & S. K. Johnson (Eds.), *Building stronger school counseling programs: Bringing futuristic approaches into the present* (pp. 37–49). Greensboro, NC: ERIC Counseling and Student Services Clearinghouse.

Bemak, F., & Chung, R. C.-Y. (2003). Multicultural counseling with immigrant students in schools. In P. B. Pedersen & J. C. Carey (Eds.), *Multicultural counseling in schools* (2nd ed., pp. 84–104). Boston: Allyn and Bacon.

Bordas, J. (2007). *Salsa, soul, and spirit: Leadership for a multicultural age*. San Francisco: Berrett-Koehler Publishers, Inc.

Brookover, W., & Erickson, E. (1969). *The trouble with Black boys: The role and influence of environmental and cultural factors on the academic performance of African American males*. East Lansing, MI: Michigan State University Press.

Brown, D. F. (2004). Urban teachers' professed classroom management strategies: Reflections of culturally responsive teaching. *Urban Education, 39*(3), 266–289.

Brown, M. C., II. (2013). The declining significance of historically Black colleges and universities: Relevance, reputation, and reality in Obamamerica. *The Journal of Negro Education, 82*(1), 3–19.

Brown, M. C., & Davis, J. E. (2001). The historically Black college as social contract, social capital, and social equalizer. *Peabody Journal of Education, 76*(1), 31–49.

Cambron-McCabe, N., & McCarthy, M. M. (2005). Educating school leaders for social justice. *Educational Policy, 19*(1), 201–222.

Cannon, K. G. (1988). *Black womanist ethics*. Atlanta: Scholars Press.

Coaxum, J., III. (2001). The misalignment between the Carnegie classifications and Black colleges. *Urban Education, 36*(5), 572–584.

Collins, P. H. (1990). *Black feminist thought: Knowledge, consciousness, and the politics of empowerment*. New York: Routledge, Chapmen, and Hall.
Collins, P. H. (1991). On our own terms: Self defined standpoints and curriculum transformation. *NWSA Journal, 3*(3), 367–381.
Conger, J. A., & Kanungo, R. A. (1988). *Charismatic leadership: The elusive factor in organization effectiveness*. San Francisco: Jossey-Bass.
Cooper, Anna Julia. (1892). Anna Julia Cooper papers, Moorland-Springarn Research Center, Howard University, Washington, D.C.
Cooper, P. M. (2003). Effective White teachers of Black children: Teaching within a community. *Journal of Teacher Education, 54*(5), 413–427.
Crenshaw, K. W. (1988). Race, reform, and retrenchment: Transformation and legitimation in anti-discrimination law. *Harvard Law Review, 101*(7), 1331–1387.
Darling-Hammond, L. (1990). Teachers and teaching: Signs of a changing profession. In W. R. Houston, M. Haberman, & J. Sikula (Eds.), *Handbook of research on teacher education* (pp. 267–290). New York: Macmillan.
Delgado, R., & Stefancic, J. (Eds.). (1997). *Critical White studies: The White race is shrinking: Perceptions of race in Canada and some speculations on the political economy of race classification*. Philadelphia: Temple University Press.
Dilworth, M. E. (1984). *Teachers totter: A report on teacher certification issues* (Occasional Paper Policy No. 6). Washington, DC: Howard University, Institute for the Study of Educational Policy.
Dryfoos, J. G. (1994). *Full-service schools: A revolution in health and social services for children, youth, and families*. San Francisco: Jossey-Bass.
Dryfoos, J. G. (1998). *Safe passage: Making it through adolescence in a risky society*. New York: Oxford University Press.
Ethridge, S. B. (1979). The impact of the 1954 Brown v. Topeka Board of Education decision on Black educators. *Negro Educational Review, 30*(4), 217–232.
Eubanks, S. C. (1996). *The urban teacher challenge: A report on teacher recruitment and demand in selected great city schools* (ERIC Document Reproduction Service No. ED400351). Belmont, MA: Recruiting New Teachers, Inc.
Ferguson, R. (1998). Can schools narrow the Black-White test score gap? In C. Jencks & M. Phillips (Eds.), *The Black-White test score gap* (pp. 318–374). Washington, DC: The Brookings Institute.
Freire, P. (1970). *Pedagogy of the oppressed*. New York: Continuum.
Futrell, M. H. (1999). Recruiting minority teachers. *Educational Leadership, 58*(8), 30–33.
Garibaldi, A. M. (1991). Abating the shortage of Black teachers. In C. V. Willie, A. M. Garibaldi, & W. L. Reed (Eds.), *The education of African-Americans* (pp. 148–158). Boston: University of Massachusetts, William Monroe Trotter Institute.
Gay, G. (2002, March/April). Preparing for culturally responsive teaching. *Journal of Teacher Education, 53*(2), 106–116.
Giddings, P. (1984). *When and where I enter the impact of Black women on race and sex in America*. New York: Bantam.
Goldhaber, D., Perry, D., & Anthony, E. (2004). The national board for professional teaching standards (NBPTS) process: Who applies and what factors are associated with NBPTS certification? *Educational Evaluation and Policy Analysis, 26*(4), 259–280.
Gurin, P., & Epps, E. (1975). *Black consciousness, identity, and achievement: A study of students in historically Black colleges*. New York: Wiley Press.
Holmes, B. (1990). *New strategies are needed to produce minority teachers* [Guest commentary] (North Central Regional Educational Laboratory Policy Briefs No. 8). Oakbrook, IL: NCREL.
Hooks, B. (2000). *Feminist theory: From margin to center* (2nd ed.). Cambridge: South End Press.

Irvine, J. J. (2002). *In search of wholeness: African American teachers and their culturally specific classroom practices.* New York: Palgrave.

Jagers, R., & Mock, L. (1993). Culture and social outcomes among inner-city African-American children: An Afrographic exploration. *Journal of Black Psychology, 19*(4), 391–405.

Jones, W. A. (2013). Prestige among Black colleges: Examining the predictors of HBCU peer academic reputation. *Journal of African American Studies, 17,* 129–141.

King, S. H. (1993). The limited presence of African American teachers. *Review of Educational Research, 63*(2), 115–149.

Ladson-Billings, G., & Tate, W. F., IV. (1995). Toward a critical race theory of education. *Teachers College Record, 97*(1), 47–68.

Lee, C. D. (2003). Why we need to re-think race and ethnicity in educational research. *Educational Researcher, 32*(5), 3–5.

Lyons, J. E., & Chesley, J. (2004). 50 years after Brown: The benefits and tradeoffs for African American educators and students. *Journal of Negro Education, 73*(3), 298–313.

Meier, K., Stewart, J., & England, R. (1989). *Race, class and education: The politics of second generation discrimination.* Madison, WI: University of Wisconsin Press.

Morris, E. W. (2007). "Ladies" or "loudies"? Perceptions and experiences of Black girls in classrooms. *Youth & Society, 38*(4), 490–515.

Morrow, R., & Torres, C. (1995). *Social theory and education.* Albany, NY: SUNY Press.

Murtadha, K., & Watts, D. M. (2005). Linking the struggle for education and social justice: Historical perspectives of African American leadership in schools. *Educational Administration Quarterly, 41*(4), 591–608.

Noguera, P. (2003). The trouble with Black boys: The role and influence of environmental and cultural factors on the academic performance of African American males. *Urban Education, 38*(4), 431–459.

Siddle-Walker, V. (1996). *Their highest potential: An African American school community in the segregated south.* Chapel Hill: University of North Carolina Press.

Sigelman, L., & Tuch, S. (1997). Meta stereotypes: Blacks' perceptions of Whites' stereotypes of Blacks. *Public Opinion Quarterly, 61*(1), 87–101.

Spencer, M. B., Swanson, D. P., & Cunningham, M. C. J. (1991). Ethnicity, ethnic identity, and competence formation: Adolescent transition and cultural transformation. *Negro Education, 60,* 367–387.

Su, Z. (1996). Why teach: Profiles and entry perspectives of minority students as becoming teachers. *Journal of Research and Development in Education, 29*(3), 117–133.

Swanson, D., Cunningham, M., & Spencer, M. B. (2003). Black males' structural conditions, achievement patterns, normative needs, and "opportunities". *Urban Education Journal, 38,* 608–633.

Theoharis, G. T. (2005, April 11–15). *Barriers to leading for social justice: The countervailing pressures public school principals face in their pursuit of equity and justice.* Paper presented at the American Education Research Association annual meeting, Montreal, Quebec, Canada.

Ware, F. (2006). Warm demander pedagogy: Culturally responsive teaching that supports a culture of achievement for African American students. *Urban Education, 41*(4), 427–456.

Wing, A. K. (Ed.). (2000). *Global critical race feminism: An international reader.* New York: New York University Press.

Witherspoon, K., Speight, S., & Thomas, A. (1997). Racial identity attitudes, school achievement, and academic self-efficacy among African American high school students. *Journal of Black Psychology, 23,* 344–357.

Wlodkowski, R. J., and Ginsberg, M. B. (1995). *Diversity and Motivation: Culturally Responsive Teaching.* San Francisco: Jossey-Bass.

6 Praise for the Bridge
My Doctoral Journey at Morgan State University

Kimberly Hardy

Telling the story of my matriculation at Morgan State University for graduate school requires understanding how I came to know and value Historically Black Colleges and Universities (HBCUs). My doctoral journey at Morgan State was truly a journey home because it laid the foundation for who and what I would become, ultimately bringing me full circle.

"It's A Different World From Where You Come From!"

At the time that I was considering life beyond high school, the television show *A Different World* premiered. The collegiate experience that played out on the fictional campus of Hillman College absolutely captivated me, from the interesting and timely topics they covered to the diversity of Black students who attended. Because commercial use of the Internet was relatively new at that time, students in my era were introduced to colleges and universities through campus visits with parents or churches and the direction of well-meaning high school guidance counselors. My parents did not attend college, my church never took a campus bus tour, and my guidance counselor never once mentioned HBCUs. Living in Maryland, I unknowingly lived in the shadow of three historically Black schools—Bowie State University, Morgan State University, and Coppin State College. I had never heard of them and never visited them, and despite their incredible histories, I never knew anything about them.

Everyone knew about the storied Black institutions of the South. Hampton, Howard, Morehouse, and Spelman were considered the Black Ivy League. Tuskegee, Grambling, and FAMU were famous for athletics and their marching bands. By and large, however, I was raised in a family that valued education regardless of the demographics, so while all of my friends packed their bags for the local state universities or campuses far away, I headed to the local community college. The campus was much more racially diverse than my high school, but most of the students were segregated into race-based social groups. At the time our experiences, all shaped by our weekly collective consumption of *A Different World*, seemed to mirror those of the show's main characters. Aside from not living in a residence hall, we were all sharing a similar storyline. In fact, the Black student athletes, with whom we had surprisingly limited interaction, called the rest of us "the Cosby Kids."

But community college is not the same—attrition is substantial in large measure because students felt like they were in "the thirteenth grade" rather than really being in college, and I was not immune to that. There was a two-year period where I was driven by youthful ignorance, believing that I could fare better in the job market without a college degree, so I dropped out of community college and became a secretary at the National Institute of Health (NIH). Over time, however, it was evident that without a college degree, the path my future would take was very limited, and this realization coincided with my growing cultural self-awareness as a Black woman. That aspect of my identity had not been cultivated; in my family, one's agency was sufficient to propel you to greater heights of attainment. Whereas my family certainly made sure that I was aware of racial bias and inequality, it was never so prominent a discussion that I came to view myself through a racialized lens. Circumstances at my community college and my secretarial position, however, made it unmistakable that race mattered and would be a nearly impossible obstacle to overcome without more education.

Several years after leaving and subsequently returning to community college, I visited Morgan State University of my own volition to interview Dr. Spencer Holland, a professor who started a program called Project 2000, which followed fifty-five African American fifth-grade students through their high school graduation. Meeting Dr. Holland was incredible. He was so inspiring, intelligent, and passionate about the work he was doing with the young people in the program. It occurred to me as I spoke to him that he was the first Black person I ever met with a doctoral degree.

When I visited Dr. Holland at Morgan, I felt like I was finally on the campus of Hillman College. Everyone looked like me, from the students and professors to the university's president. I meandered across the campus, taking in all of the tropes of Black college life I saw on television: the students in Greek letters, the archetypes of various social cliques, the crowded dining facilities, and the bookstore. The books that professors assigned for classes had titles that were provocative and content that was challenging, and almost all of them were by and about Black people. My time on campus left an incredible impression, and I knew in that moment that I would ultimately become a Morganite.

Not long after that initial visit, I connected with one of my cousins who was a student there, and she brought me to campus for a more formal tour. She introduced me to everyone she knew, including Mr. Bill Carson. Despite all of the other introductions, when she introduced me to Mr. Carson she quite earnestly stated, "If you ever need *anything*, you go see him." After I was enrolled, I sought him out immediately, and he became vitally important in my personal, academic, and professional development. To this day, Mr. Carson remains a valued friend and cherished mentor.

In truth there were many people at Morgan during my undergraduate years who were pivotal in my life. Although far too numerous to name, the faculty, staff, and administrators were like family to me, providing guidance when I lost my way and admonishment when I did not perform to their very high expectations. My first department chair, Dr. Talley, would drive me to school when I had no other way to get to campus, and the building janitor, Mr. Suggs, would drive me home at night so I would not have to walk home alone in the dark. Marsha, the department secretary, would offer Mr. Suggs five dollars each week for gas money in exchange for making the trip, and he would decline every time. Dr. Elmer Martin, one of the most esteemed professors on campus, would send me to get his lunch and *require* that I buy something for myself because he knew I would have nothing to eat otherwise.

My classmates were important to me as well. I developed friendships, formed in times of both joy and sorrow, which endure to this day. Together we cultivated supportive social networks that were especially necessary for those of us who arrived at Morgan having already claimed a few years of "real world" experience. What we found in each other was a comfort in our shared vulnerability—late bloomers, unsure about our futures, yet excited about the possibilities that lay ahead. What we found in our professors was a predetermination of our expected greatness—they had already blazed a trail through the darkness of racism and diminished expectations so that we could more easily navigate toward our dreams. What we found at Morgan was a home.

"Your Destiny is in That PhD Program at Morgan"

The decision to pursue my PhD at Morgan State University was not initially my own. Despite having had a positive experience in undergrad, Morgan did not have a graduate social work program at the time, so it was a forgone conclusion that my tenure at my alma mater would end after completing my BSW. By the time I handed in my admission packet for the doctoral program many years later, I had earned my MSW from the Ohio State University, worked as a school social worker in several major cities, endured a very challenging few years in a doctoral program at the University of Chicago, and returned home to Maryland, where I would unknowingly spend one last year with my mother before she lost her battle to cancer.

I was in the throes of so much confusion and turbulence at the time that I returned home, but I was excited to learn that Morgan had finally started their own MSW program. When I contacted the department chair, Dr. Anna McPhatter, who had been a wonderful mentor to me during my BSW program, to ask about teaching a few courses, she told me that they were starting a PhD in the fall and encouraged me to apply. After the anguish of my experience at Chicago, my spirit was broken and my confidence shaken. I had no intention of enrolling in another doctoral program . . . not even at Morgan. But during a routine overnight hospital stay I visited my mother, and she told me, "Your destiny is in that PhD program at Morgan." Borrowing from her confidence, I decided to apply. No sooner had I begun to prepare my application materials, my mother passed away. The grief was unbearable, and I lost all of my motivation to finish the process; I began simply going through the motions. In fact, I waited so long to apply that I had to hand-deliver my application package to Dr. McPhatter directly. The application process was thorny and complicated, but I persevered largely on the encouragement of my mother's words and was ultimately admitted into the inaugural cohort of the social work PhD program . . . a moniker that would be a blessing and a challenge over the next four years.

"People Love That for Which They Labor, and They Labor for That Which They Love"

Despite unfounded yet no less popular belief, the educational program at an HBCU is incredibly rigorous, and I was fortunate to have walked in the door knowing that my doctoral program would not belie my baccalaureate experience. Academically, the work was significantly more rigorous than had been the case in my program at Chicago, where I was only required to take two ten-week statistics courses. Morgan's PhD program, by contrast, required three fifteen-week quantitative statistics courses, a qualitative research course, and a research methods course. One of our statistics professors, Dr. Harold Aubrey, literally knew the story of how feuds between several prominent statistical pioneers led to the creation of near-similar statistical procedures that are still commonly used in research. Our professor for social welfare policy, Dr. Jay Carrington Chunn, mentioned a book on our topic of discussion in class one night and told us that we should read it. The following week when we stared at him sheepishly as he asked us what we thought of the book, we were reprimanded intensely for not realizing that he was not suggesting we read the book that week but requiring it. Our professors were pioneers in the field of social work, scholars who were the first Black Americans to earn doctorates from their respective institutions, and great intellectuals whose research was not bound to their vita, but conducted in service to the broader Black community. We were exposed to all of the traditional social scientific theoretical frameworks for explaining and predicting various social phenomena, yet we were also taught about the Afrocentric paradigm as an equally viable and more culturally -relevant lens through which to understand the lived experiences of those who stood to benefit the most from our research efforts. We were exposed to the great intellectual minds of Plato, Robert Merton, and Na'im Akbar.

We were all required to work hard, think deeply, and support our arguments with solid scholarly evidence. I was pushed harder at Morgan than I was at Chicago and Ohio State; more was expected of me, required of me, because my success or failure had community consequences. What I did not produce meant there would be lack for those whose pain could only be healed by the work I needed to do. The journey of my classmates and me was not unique in this way. Ed Bradley, a graduate of Cheyney, said, "There were always professors who would encourage students to do better; professors who would demand more. And there were so many who encouraged you to be the best you could be" (pg. xxiv).

The notion of some that a Black college education is less valuable than one earned at a traditionally White institution is not only wholly inaccurate but evidences the wholesale consumption of a narrative designed to diminish the significance of our institutions. The data, however, refute that narrative when one considers that the most prominent Black figures in the history of this country were groomed for those leadership positions in the halls of HBCUs. The list ranges from scholars to artists, athletes to executives, pastors to politicians, educators to engineers: Rev. Ralph David Abernathy (Alabama State), Alice Walker (Spelman), Barbara Jordan (Texas Southern), Spike Lee (Morehouse), Earl G. Graves (Morgan), Toni Morrison (Howard), John W. Thompson (Florida A&M), and many others. The way forward from the mire of racism and oppression to the mountaintop of justice and freedom for Blacks has always been education, and as journalist Juan Williams said, "Only one set of institutions in American history has made delivering education to Black people their central mission—the historically black colleges and universities" (Williams & Ashley, xvii).

Positive Experiences

Some of the most positive experiences I had during my doctoral studies at Morgan State took place outside of the classroom. Several in particular stand out because of the impact they had on others and me. For instance, I had the opportunity to serve as the president of the Graduate Student Association (GSA). The fledgling group had done good work in the past but had established little traction at the time of my appointment. Although it would take a great deal of work and university resources, I was given permission to have the GSA host an academic conference at Morgan for Black graduate students across the country. The conference was an incredible success as it brought budding scholars together at an HBCU to showcase their work to peers, network with future colleagues, and do so in a spirit of support and encouragement. Years later I was part of a larger group e-mail with scholars from various universities and was able to reconnect with a woman who had presented at the conference. She talked about how positive the experience had been for her to share her research with people who were cheering her on rather than looking for flaws.

Another positive experience was the consequence of uncontemplated zealousness. Believing myself ready for the "big leagues" of academic life, I submitted an abstract for a paper presentation to a conference in California. I was selected, which was exciting and frightening, and the dean of the Graduate School provided the funds for me to attend. Conspicuously omitting the details of the crushing anxiety I felt before I presented, I apparently did very well for my first solo conference presentation. I learned so much about how to present research, how to project confidence, and how to handle combative audience members—all of which would prove rather important for my dissertation defense. Those points notwithstanding, the real reason this experience was positive was because I met other scholars in my research area of spirituality and social work practice who continue to be dear friends and colleagues to this day. One of them, Dr. Taqi Tirmazi, would actually join the Morgan faculty as a Kellogg post-doc fellow the following year and ultimately serve as the research methodologist for my dissertation.

Whereas neither of these experiences were unique to having attended an HBCU for graduate school, they reflect for me the university's belief and investment in my leadership and scholarship. I was encouraged to think creatively and act boldly in an environment that was willing to support my efforts no matter the outcome; this was not the case in my previous doctoral program. It has not been the case for my Black American peers who pursued their doctorate in traditionally White universities where competition among colleagues is sponsored like a sport and where constant microaggressions make them question the veracity of both their scholarship and their personhood. They are frequently the only Black Americans in their cohort, as was my case at Chicago, and their inability to understand concepts that others appeared to master easily not only incited self-doubt but isolation as they detached from others to hide what they saw as their academic shortcomings. I know that experience firsthand, and it can be a spirit-damaging reality. However, I went from barely grasping my initial statistics classes at Chicago to running the advanced statistics study group for my peers. Even now I help colleagues understand basic statistical procedures when they are designing research projects, and I teach the students in my research and statistics classes in the way I wish my professors had taught it to me. Such a significant transformation can only happen in a learning community where you believe you can fall safely but where you are supported so that you never do.

"You Praise the Bridge That Carried You Across"

My mother used to tell my brothers and me all the time that you praise the bridge that carried you across. She wanted us to understand the value in the process of going through no matter how challenging that process may have been and to honor the process for moving you from one side of a situation to the other. Given that, I am naturally inclined toward a strengths-based perspective on most issues and am loathe to consider any of my experiences in the doctoral program as negative. I choose rather to cast them in the context of the common fits and starts associated with establishing a new academic program. The learning curve is substantial when you are doing something for the first time, and that was certainly true for those of us in the inaugural doctoral cohort. Every misstep or oversight made the deepest cut in my classmates as the faculty and administrators grappled with the frequent need to course correct. Every class that was taught, lecture given, and policy enacted was initiated for the first time on us, serving only to exacerbate both the natural anxiety of doctoral education and the heightened expectations of professors whose personal example of excellence often felt impossible to emulate. Although many of those fits and starts were frustrating, they were not wholly negative because the faculty valued our perspective enough to listen to us when making changes to the program that would benefit us and the cohorts enrolled in subsequent years.

Career Preparation

My doctoral journey at Morgan prepared me for life in academia in a plethora of ways—some of which were surprising. For instance, although I could never have anticipated it at the time, the challenges faced by the faculty and administration in bringing the new PhD program to life have been invaluable to the work I am doing now in creating a new MSW program at my current university. Crafting syllabi and structuring courses that are solid, rigorous, and inspiring on paper yet fall flat in their execution in the classroom has been humbling. However, I am convinced that my Morgan professors, listening to and valuing the feedback that we gave them as students, made me more sensitive to the disquiet among my students about what needed to change so that our program could prepare them for success. Morgan taught me how to engage the students in the process of strengthening the program, remembering that their contributions were no less valuable than those of the professors. I also learned to see the fits and starts as part of the process that would help us all grow rather than as a series of failures and missteps.

Morgan taught me that the purpose of my scholarship is not to populate my curriculum vitae or achieve prominence as a public intellectual but to be a tool in service of those living in isolated, under-resourced communities regardless of their racial background. Community-engaged research is not about serving on a board of directors but rather about promoting justice and equity for people whose socially constructed identities cause them to languish on society's margins.

Perhaps more than anything, however, Morgan taught me to ensure the success of my Black students. College classrooms are the four-walled fiefdoms of professors, and I recognize the power that my intervention—or lack thereof—can have on the students in my charge. Whereas I am invested in the success of all of my students, my advocacy on behalf of Black students takes on special meaning for me. I have fed the ones who were hungry, guided the ones who were struggling, admonished the ones who were flailing, and celebrated them all when they succeeded. I want someone like Dr. Talley, Dr. Martin, Dr. McPhatter, Mr. Carson, Mr. Suggs, and Marsha to take care of my son when he enrolls in college one day, and every Black student I have has someone at home hoping the same for their child. They sent their sons and daughters to me with prayers but very little else, and I see it as my responsibility to push them and care for them in ways that most of their other professors never will because they either do not care or they do not understand. More than once I have been greeted with outstretched arms by parents, grandparents, aunts, and older siblings after commencement who whisper, "Thank you for taking care of my baby" or a chorus of, "So *you're* Dr. Hardy!" It is in those private moments that I am affirmed in the work I have done because that moment has literally changed the narrative of this family's history. And when the pomp and circumstance have ended, I do not leave them. Morgan taught me the profound value of mentorship, and just as I continue to reach out to those who helped guide me get to this place, I continue to lift my now-former students as I climb.

Advice/Recommendations

No matter which school you attend or which degree you pursue, if you attend an HBCU, you know that homecoming is the most anticipated weekend of the year. The pageantry of the parade, the battle of the bands at halftime, the vendors hawking their wares, the tailgating, reconnecting with old friends—there is no experience like it anywhere. The campus is at its manicured best to spark envy in the visiting team and pride among the alumni. Neophyte fraternity and sorority members wearing every piece of paraphernalia they were gifted stroll through campus alongside their graying older members. Homecoming reminds you that there is always a place for you to retreat to where memories live on and you are always welcomed, valued, needed.

In the wake of an unprecedented number of police-involved killings of Black Americans for trivial infractions at best and blatant lies at worst, it strikes me that a homecoming is required in the community. Black graduate students need to come home to the HBCU so that they can thrive under the watchful eye of other Black scholars who are devoted to their development as they work toward solutions to problems of social science and natural science. Black graduate students need to come to a place where their contributions are welcomed, their personhood valued, their ideas needed. The Black community is being assaulted in ways that hearken back to the black-and-white photographs of the civil rights movement; scholars and critics like Michelle Alexander and Ta-Nehisi Coates are sounding the call for our greatest minds to commit themselves to social justice and community uplift. HBCUs have always been leaders in the movement for racial justice and equal rights either through protest marches and boycotts or preparing scientists, scholars, and educators who challenge the status quo. What one gains from attending graduate school at an HBCU is the playbook the community once used to achieve freedom and support to create the next chapter.

Aside from what some may see as macro-level justice and equality bombast, one does also gain something else from graduate education at an HBCU—an unequivocal confidence in your academic preparation and a broader diversity of thought through exposure to an entire population of scholars and literatures that are routinely disregarded. You will know your content as well as those who taught it to you because they will ensure that you are prepared for the doubtful looks and second-guesses. You will be unapologetic about your Black presence in White spaces, and you will challenge them to be critically self-reflective about what they believe. You will gain a sense of place and identity as a Black intellectual and professional as you push forward toward the realization that *you* are "the hope and the dream of the slave."

7 Free to Conduct Research of Race and Racism in My West Baltimore Community

Julius Davis

The murder of Freddie Gray, a twenty-five-year-old Black man, brought issues of race and racism to the forefront of the lived realities and schooling of Black adults and children in West Baltimore. Before Gray's murder, my experiences living in poor and working class Black communities in West Baltimore led me to study how issues of race and racism shaped the lived realities, schooling, and mathematics education of Black students. I engaged in such research because I felt a sense of responsibility to my community and race. I also wanted to conduct research about my community at a Black institution that was significant to me and my family; thus, the reason I attended Morgan State University (MSU), an urban Historically Black College and University (HBCU). The institution and faculty provided me with a supportive intellectual space to conduct what I consider to be liberatory research (Martin, 2009).

In this chapter, I describe how my family and mentors influenced my decision to attend Historically Black Colleges and Universities (HBCUs). Then, I describe my experiences studying issues of race and racism at Morgan State University and the support Black faculty and graduate students provided me. Afterward, I describe my post-doctoral experience and tenure track faculty positions and how they helped to create new lines of research and opportunities to serve my community. I conclude by offering advice to graduate students studying at HBCUs and clarify important points.

Family Influence Decision to Attend an HBCU

My decision to attend MSU for my graduate studies started long before I decided to pursue a doctoral degree in mathematics education. I had family members who attended Morgan that shaped my decision to attend the institution. Extant literature has provided evidence that family members can play a significant role in shaping Black students' majors in college (Davis, Jones, & Clark, 2013; Foster, 1997). However, little is known about how family members influence Black students' decision to pursue graduate degrees. My father and aunt attended Morgan as undergrads; he was studying to be a teacher, and my aunt was studying to be a social worker. My father was a student athlete who played football for Morgan and did not complete his studies or earn a degree. He did, however, learn many life lessons and met many people who positively shaped his life to this day. He passed those lessons on to me.

Growing up, my father was an avid supporter of HBCUs, and he transferred his love for the institutions down to me. He talked about the value of HBCUs and supporting the institutions on a regular basis. My father wanted his children to attend HBCUs. Three out of his five children attended and earned bachelor's degrees from HBCUs. Two of them have earned degrees at Morgan. My love for HBCUs played a major role in my decision to attend and earn my bachelor of science degree in mathematics education from Lincoln University of Pennsylvania, the first HBCU in the United States.

Mentor Influence Decision to Attend an HBCU

At Lincoln, I was mentored and studied under the late world-renowned mathematician Dr. Abdulalim Abdullah Shabazz, who was also an alumnus of the institution. Before his passing, Dr. Shabazz was credited with being responsible for the majority of Blacks with a doctoral degree in mathematics (and mathematics education) fields (Hilliard, 1995). Dr. Shabazz was the first person to expose me the contributions to mathematics of people of African descent. Under his tutelage, I was exposed to and encouraged to attend graduate school. Dr. Shabazz exposed me to national mathematics organizations and conferences that focused on encouraging Black students to pursue graduate degrees in mathematics and mathematics education fields. He exposed me to Black graduate students at different levels and Black faculty members in mathematics and mathematics education around the country.

Dr. Shabazz expanded my conceptualization of what it means to do and study mathematics and use mathematics in the service of my community and race. The mentorship I received in undergrad by Dr. Shabazz and others led me to the conclusion that I wanted to earn a doctorate in mathematics education to give back to my community and race. In undergrad, my mentors and professors encouraged me to go directly to graduate school and continue my studies after graduating. The preparation I received from Lincoln made me feel that I could accomplish anything that I put my mind to. I left the university feeling prepared for the challenges of graduate school and any other task put in front of me.

My research of graduate schools started with HBCUs, but very few of them have doctoral programs in mathematics education. I was fortunate that Morgan State University's School of Education and Urban Studies had a doctoral program in mathematics education. I applied and was accepted into the graduate programs for mathematics and science education with a fellowship. In many respects, attending Morgan was a way for me to earn a degree that my father never got to obtain. Surprisingly, my middle school science teacher was a student in the program and in my first class. She was one of the most supportive people during my doctoral studies. A few years into my doctoral studies, my high school mathematics teacher joined the faculty in the program, guided my dissertation, served as the chairperson of my committee, and helped me earn my doctoral degree in mathematics education.

Studying Issues of Race and Racism at Morgan

When I started my studies at Morgan, I knew I wanted to conduct research of how issues of race and racism impacted the lived realities, schooling, and mathematics education of Black students in my West Baltimore community. However, I did not know exactly how I was going to conduct such research and if Morgan was a safe space to do so. I was a little concerned about how I was going to conduct my research because of past experiences in undergraduate fighting against issues of race and racism and being retaliated against by faculty members and administrators. During my first semester in the doctoral program, a Black male faculty member assured me that I was in a safe space to conduct research of race and racism. I remember the day when my professor pulled me aside after class and said:

> Julius, it seems like you want to focus on issues of race and racism, but you are hesitant. I want to let you know that Morgan is a safe space to do this type of work, and that's why I came to the university.

I thanked my professor and reflected on his words. I must admit, I was a little reluctant to trust his words but decided to do so after careful thought and consideration. Trusting his advice was one of the best decisions I made in graduate school. He continues to play a major role in my development as a man and scholar. Ture and Hamilton (1992) argue:

> Those who would assume the responsibility of representing black people in this country must be able to throw off the notion that they can effectively do so and still maintain a maximum amount of security. Jobs will have to be sacrificed, positions of prestige and status given up, favors forfeited . . . When one forcefully challenges the racist system, one cannot, at the same time, expect that system to reward him or even treat him comfortably.
>
> (p. 15)

After reflecting and talking with my professor, I realized that I can conduct research of race and racism and expect to be comfortable doing so. My mentors and past experiences made that clear to me. From that point, I fully committed to my research and used every opportunity in my doctoral classes to conceptualize different aspects of my study. I used classes to explore my definitions and conceptualizations of race and racism, conduct pilot studies to flush out my participants, research questions and methodology, and explore different theoretical frameworks.

Black Faculty and Graduate Students' Support of My Research and Development

Throughout my doctoral studies, I got support from Black faculty members and covert and overt disdain from some White faculty members. Take, for instance, faculty deliberations about my comprehensive exam, a White faculty member tried to make a case that I did not need to focus on issues of race and racism in the lives of Black students because things were not as bad for them as I had indicated in my papers. A Black faculty member disagreed with the White faculty member and defended my focus and asked the White faculty member to offer suggestions or research to help me rethink my position. However, the White faculty member did not have any suggestions or research to offer. This instance was indicative of my experience with the White faculty member in her class. She always presented opposition to my focus on racism in her class.

During my doctoral studies, my development as a scholar was enhanced by Black faculty members, senior Black graduate students, and exposure to the larger educational research community. The Black faculty members at Morgan taught me how to develop my research agenda. Doctoral students and faculty members attended and presented at national conferences together. Morgan provided me with a community of faculty and doctoral student scholars to help me develop my ideas, push my thinking, and challenge my thoughts and beliefs and helped me figure out how to navigate the program and academy. One of the senior graduate students served as a mentor to help me navigate through the program and served as a critical reviewer, offering salient feedback to help improve my papers.

Writing My Paper for AERA Annual Conference

A year into my doctoral studies, I submitted a proposal to the American Educational Research Association (AERA) for consideration at the annual conference. The proposal was accepted, which meant that I had to write a paper to present at the conference. Writing this paper played a major role in my development as a scholar. My graduate student mentor read a draft of the paper and provided me with feedback that suggested the ideas presented in my paper could be used to develop multiple papers. In other words, I needed to narrow my focus in the paper to a set of core ideas and use the other ideas for other papers. I considered contacting AERA to inform them that I would not be presenting my paper until I spoke to my trusted Black male professor, who convinced me that I needed to get myself together and complete the paper in order to present. My experience writing that paper was a transformative experience and an important part of my development as a scholar.

My Scholarly Development at AERA Annual Conference

Not only was writing the paper transformative, but attending and presenting at the annual AERA conference was too. Faculty members served as cultural guides at the conference and taught me and other graduate students how to navigate the conference. They also taught us that our scholarship is supposed to make a contribution to the larger educational research community. Faculty members used the conference to extend their teaching from the classroom. The conference exposed me to the larger educational community and allowed me to meet junior and senior scholars in my field and further develop my ideas by attending sessions focused on my interests and area of research. It was at AERA that I met a senior scholar who was an expert in critical race theory, and I developed a relationship with him and asked him to be a member of my dissertation committee. This scholar played a major role in shaping my doctoral dissertation by providing expertise on critical race theory and suggesting that I use critical ethnography as the methodology for my study.

Interacting With Senior Black Scholars at a Colloquium

Later in my academic career at a colloquium, I was conversing with two senior Black scholars, and I was advised not to conduct research of race and racism until I got tenure. One of the senior Black scholars was opposed to the idea and advised against waiting to conduct research of such important issues until I received tenure. He was actually the same scholar who served on my dissertation committee and played a major role in my development as a mathematics educator who uses critical race theory in my research. In my view, it is important for Black graduate students to conduct research of race and racism and other important topics as doctoral students because dissertations serve as the foundation for the development of your research agenda.

Doctoral Student Publication

Another important aspect of my development as a scholar was publishing as a doctoral student. My first publication was with a senior Black scholar in the field focused on racism, assessment, and instructional practices used for Black students in mathematics education (Davis & Martin, 2008). This article was a compilation of ideas from my dissertation and his research, scholarship, experiences, and observations of how issues of race, racism, assessment, and instructional practices impacted the mathematics education of Black students. Similar to my experiences with the AERA paper, writing my first article with a senior scholar in the field resulted in similar feedback. My ideas and thoughts were all over the place, and he helped me to refocus my ideas. This experience was critical to my development of what it takes to prepare a quality article for publication and complete my dissertation.

My Dissertation: Studying the Impact of Oppression on Black Middle School Students

My dissertation focused on the lived realities, schooling, and mathematics education of Black middle school students in my West Baltimore community. I used critical race theory and critical ethnography to examine how issues of race, racism, classism, and other forms of oppression shaped their experiences. I captured the experiences of six Black middle school students and fifteen ethnographic snapshots of other Black middle school students to describe how issues of race, racism, and other forms of oppression shaped their lived realities, schooling, and mathematics education. To show how these issues impacted the students, I used critical race theory's notion of revisionist history to reexamine the lived realities, schooling, and mathematics education of Black adults and children in Baltimore.

The revisionist history and results of my study shed light into the same issues impacting Freddie Gray and our West Baltimore community. Black students (and their families) received poor-quality schooling that led to compounded economic conditions that shaped families and the community. The themes resulting from my study were institutionalized confinement, cultural agency, participatory oppression, and debilitating mathematics education. These themes suggest that the conditions in Black communities and schools were intended to keep Black students and adults subordinate in order to maintain White supremacy. Another salient result was that Black males, like Freddie Gray, were the most subjugated in classrooms, schools, and the community.

Post-Doctoral Experience: The Development of a New Line of Research

In my view, studying Black mathematics teachers was a logical extension of my research of Black students. My research agenda was expanded with a post-doctoral experience in the Center for Mathematics Education (CfME) at the University of Maryland, College Park. I strongly believe that my preparation at Morgan played a major role in helping me to secure and be prepared for the post-doctoral experience. In the CfME, I was provided the opportunity to join the Case Studies of Urban Algebra I Teachers research team. The team was comprised of university faculty, post-doctoral students, and doctoral students. The research was funded by the National Science Foundation (NSF) and focused on studying Black Algebra I teachers' educational and professional experiences and praxis. I was mentored by a Black faculty member who also benefited from attending an HBCU as an undergrad.

The post-doctoral experience provided me with an opportunity to engage in in-depth study of the educational and professional experiences and praxis of Black mathematics teachers in urban settings. It also provided me with the opportunity to learn more about grant writing and managing them. Furthermore, it provided me with an insider view of how doctoral students at a predominantly White institution were prepared to be researchers. I was able to develop a new line of research focused on Black mathematics teachers with emphasis on Black male teachers. This experience resulted in national presentations and publications in a top-tiered journal (Clark, Frank, & Davis, 2013) and book chapter (Davis et al., 2013) in an important book on Black male teachers.

Giving Back: Tenure Track Position at an HBCU

My doctoral studies and post-doctoral experience helped prepare me for a tenure track position at Bowie State University, the oldest HBCU in the state of Maryland. My decision to teach at Bowie was a direct reflection of my upbringing, love for HBCUs, and influence of mentors, faculty, and graduate students who helped me to develop into a man and scholar. One of the main reasons I wanted to work at an HBCU was to give back to community. Being a faculty member allows me to share my experiences and knowledge with Black students who are developing into men and women and teach them the importance of using their education for the uplift of the Black community. Most of my undergraduate mentors were alumni of Lincoln University, and they were committed to uplifting Black people and returning to the university to support the institution. My decision to teach at Bowie is following in their footsteps.

The Attack on HBCUs

Another reason I decided to teach at Bowie revolves around the attack on HBCUs. Despite the rhetoric about diversifying the nation's workforce, HBCUs are under attack at every level, including recruitment and retention, federal and state funding, endowments, student financial assistance (Pell grant, parent plus loan, etc.), oppressive policies, and accreditation processes. I have gotten involved in the accreditation process to learn more about how these processes impact HBCUs. First off, HBCUs have to put up a large sum of money that is not regularly available to go through the accreditation process. The money does not remain after the process is over to improve areas needing improvement. Second, there are not many people knowledgeable on the accreditation process and standards to implement the necessary requirements, analyze data, and write the reports. At HBCUs, faculty are often overburdened by the heavy teaching, advising, and service loads coupled with the increasing research and grant-writing requirements. Contributing to the accreditation process is another element of faculty workloads at HBCUs that is not fully considered. HBCUs need faculty (and administrators) who are knowledgeable and willing to contribute to the accreditation process and keep active research and grant-writing agendas to help keep the institutions in operation. It bothers me that my undergraduate university, Lincoln, lost its undergraduate teacher education program through the accreditation process.

HBCUs' Contribution to Diversifying the Nation's Workforce

HBCUs have made major contributions to diversifying the nation's workforce long before the idea became popular. HBCUs have played a major role in producing Blacks with undergraduate and graduate degrees. The US Department of Education has targeted HBCUs as sites to push the Teach Campaign, a federal policy initiative designed to diversify the nation's teaching profession and increase the number of Blacks in the profession. HBCUs produce half of the Black K–12 teachers; however, the support needed for the institutions and future teachers have not followed the initiative. The US Government and Department of Education, state and local agencies and businesses have been calling for more science, technology, engineering, and mathematics (STEM) professionals and to diversify that workforce. HBCUs produce 40 percent of the nation's STEM graduates, and a disproportionate number of the Blacks who earn PhDs in STEM fields attended HBCUs as undergraduates. Many Black students have been cultivated into great men and women because of self-knowledge, experiences, teaching, and supportive environments received at HBCUs. With these contributions and more, there are many politicians, policymakers, and philanthropists who question the relevance of HBCUs despite the contributions of Blacks to the nation.

My Black Male Research and Service Agenda

With the attack on HBCUs and Black boys and young men, like Freddie Gray, I have expanded my research agenda at Bowie to include Black male college students, Black male pre- and in-service teachers, and Black mathematics teachers. I have also developed a service component to complement my research agenda focused on Black male students throughout the K–16 pipeline. I also continue to conduct research of and serve Black males throughout the K–12 pipeline. I strongly believe that Black scholars' research/scholarship of our people and community must include a service component to improve our collective conditions. Being a faculty member at Bowie has provided me with access to Black males from diverse backgrounds to study and shape their knowledge, experiences, careers, and perspective of our collective issues as a people and views of the world. As a part of my service to Black males, I have played a major role in Bowie's male initiative and created programs for Black males in public and private schools as well as an African-centered school. My programs have served Black males in adjudication programs, public school and community-based mentoring programs, job corps, and foster homes.

Advice for Graduate Students Studying at HBCUs

Since I was a graduate student, many things have changed; especially the expectations for graduate students coming out of doctoral programs. I once attended an AERA session focused on publications facilitated by Dr. Gloria Ladson-Billings (an undergraduate Morgan State University alumna) who discussed how graduate students from research one universities were leaving graduate school with five or more publications and a host of presentations. Many of the graduate students at research one universities are a part of research teams, like the one I participated in at the University of Maryland, and benefit from the collaborative publication and presentation opportunities with faculty.

Graduate students should enter graduate school with a research topic (or develop one within the first year of the program) that they do not change and then use their courses to further develop their dissertation research. Graduate students should find a faculty mentor who conducts research on their area of interest to help guide their research/faculty career. Graduate students should find a senior graduate student or post-doctoral research associate to help navigate them through their doctoral program, the larger educational community, presentations, and publications. Graduate students should create publications and develop presentations that are aligned with their research agenda as graduate students. I would also strongly encourage Black graduate students to conduct research that is important to the Black community and use methodologies and frameworks that are culturally sensitive and/or challenge systems of oppression and deficit perspectives of our people (Tillman, 2002). I would also strongly encourage Black graduate students to develop a service agenda that complements their research agenda. Graduate students also need a scholarly community to share and develop ideas, push their thinking, challenge their thoughts and beliefs, help them develop a solid research and service agenda, and figure out how to navigate their studies and academy. Finally, I would encourage graduate students to engage in a post-doctoral experience to further develop their research agenda before becoming a tenure track faculty member at a university.

Conclusion

My undergraduate and doctoral experiences at HBCUs were instrumental to my development as a man and Black scholar educator with sociopolitical consciousness and self-knowledge. My love for HBCUs, sociopolitical consciousness, and self-knowledge started with my family but was enhanced at both my HBCU experiences. I was taught by my family, mentors, professors, and peers that I have a responsibility to use my education for the benefit of my family, community, and race. In my view, Black scholars have a responsibility to conduct meaningful research that will help to shed light on the problems impacting the larger Black community and develop solutions to those problems. I have focused my research and service to the Black community on empowering and uplifting Black children, especially Black males.

I use my position as an assistant professor at an HBCU to serve Black males at Bowie and the surrounding community. I strongly believe that HBCUs have to take a lead role in supporting Black boys and young men in our community, like Freddie Gray and so many others (Davis, Land, & Parker, 2014). My focus on Black males stems from findings from dissertation research and the larger body of literature that describes their successes and challenges. In doing this work, I was able to complete a degree at Morgan that my father was not able to earn. The Black community needs more scholars with advanced degrees to use their knowledge to uplift, enhance, and improve our collective conditions. Our conditions require that Black people take responsibility for finding solutions to our problems to liberate our people and become self-reliant.

References

Clark, L., Frank, T., & Davis, J. (2013). Conceptualizing the African American mathematics teacher as a key figure in the African American education historical narrative. *Teachers College Record, 115*(2), 1–29.

Davis, J., Jones, T., & Clark, L. (2013). The case of a Black male mathematics teacher teaching in a unique urban context: Implications for recruiting Black male mathematics teachers. In C. W. Lewis & I. A. Toldson (Eds.), *Black male teachers: Diversifying the nation's workforce* (pp. 77–92). Bingley, UK: Emerald Group Publishing.

Davis, J., Land, O., & Parker, W. (2014, December). My brother's keeper: The role of HBCUs in providing support for African American men. *Diverse: Issues in Higher Education*. Retrieved from http://diverseeducation.com/article/68472/

Davis, J., & Martin, D. B. (2008). Racism, assessment & instructional practices: Implications for mathematics teachers of African American students. *Journal of Urban Mathematics Education, 1*(1), 10–34.

Foster, M. (1997). *Black teachers on teaching*. New York, NY: Carroll & Graf Publishers.

Hilliard, A. (1995). *The maroon within us: Select essays of African American socialization*. Baltimore, MD: Black Classic Press.

Martin, D. B. (2009). Liberating the production of knowledge about African-American children and mathematics. In D. Martin (Ed.), *Mathematics teaching, learning and liberation in the lives of Black children* (pp. 3–38). London: Routledge.

Tillman, L. (2002). Culturally sensitive research approaches: An African American perspective. *Educational Researcher, 31*(9), 3–12.

Ture, K., & Hamilton, C. V. (1992). *Black power: The politics of liberation*. New York, NY: Vintage Books.

8 The Historically Black College and University Family
A Perspective on a Graduate-Level Online Accelerated Cohort Program

Kimberly R. Eldridge

Limited research focuses on the perspectives of graduate-level students in online programs (Kumar & Dawson, 2012). This chapter will focus on the student viewpoint of an accelerated online cohort PhD program at an Historically Black College and University (HBCU) in the southern region of the United States. For this chapter, the author will share her personal perspective and include cohort members' narratives. The author will guide you through the doctoral process while providing advice.

Seeking a higher education was an expectation growing up in my household. My parents were both first-generation college students. They set the precedent on the importance of achieving academically and being a good steward of the community. After receiving both my bachelor's and master's degree from predominantly White institutions (PWIs), attending an HBCU for my doctoral work was one of my goals. During my doctoral research, I decided that an HBCU would add value to my academic career because of the rich tradition and the opportunity to study with minority colleagues.

Motivation to Pursue a Graduate Degree at an HBCU

Several factors motivated me to attend an online doctoral program with a cohort model at an HBCU. The factors are as follows: (1) The ability to work a full-time job while pursuing the graduate degree; (2) the convenience of having academic courses online; (3) attending and graduating from an institution where majority of the students come from diverse populations; and (4) my career goal is to become a college president. As an educator, educating students on the K–12 level and in higher education, I have always been motivated to work with diverse student populations. Providing programs and services to help students navigate higher education through access, graduation completion, and beyond is quite rewarding.

Online and Cohort Experience

Fuller, Risner, Lowder, Hart, and Bachenheimer (2014, p. 74) suggest that three principal elements to successful development of online learning environments are "social presence, cognitive presence, and teaching presence." Garrison and Arbaugh (2007) express that social presence in an online environment allows the student to connect to other students socially and emotionally, providing cohesiveness among the group. This nurtures the sense of community and contributes to the positive online learning experience. How "students progress from understanding, to exploration, to integration to application encouraging through in-depth discussions is cognitive presence" (Fuller et al., 2014, p. 75). "Teaching presence is the instructional design that enhances both the social and the cognitive presences" (Fuller et al., 2014, p. 75).

Cohort-based learning has existed in higher education since the 1990s (Rausch & Crawford, 2012). Bista and Cox (2014, p. 4) suggest that the "cohort based model fosters a dynamics of group cohesion." "The cohort learning model promotes academic rigor, establishes socially supportive relationships among students as they move toward completion" (Rausch & Crawford, 2012, p. 175).

Starting an online program gave me some anxiety. In my master's program, I had a few online classes but did not receive feedback. Experiencing this made me a little apprehensive about this program. After my research, I decided that this program would suit me well. When taking online classes, I was intentional in how I built relationships with staff and professors.

Having a cohort model experience was very beneficial for me. Working with seven colleagues during the academic process nurtured a "family" environment. I became the designated leader of the cohort and facilitated weekly conference calls to discuss assignments. Texting was a daily routine to stay abreast of issues that may have arisen. After completing the required coursework, communication with my cohort dwindled. During the dissertation phase, communications with my cohort members rarely garnered responses. It seemed as if my cohort members did not want to communicate about their process in the dissertation phase. This saddened me; I loved to encourage my cohort, but it felt like I lost my family as I continued through the process. When the communication dwindled, it felt very lonely. I come to understand everyone was committed to his or her individual dissertation, and it consumed their time. I did, however, pay it forward by encouraging and mentoring cohort members who came before and after my cohort.

Residency Experience

The cohort started the program at the residency stage in summer 2011; there was a total of eleven cohort members, but it decreased to eight the second semester. The cohort was afforded the opportunity to start the program face-to-face with professors. Having the opportunity to start the program face-to-face gave the cohort an opportunity to bond and build relationships with our professors and potential committee members for our dissertation.

During the first residency, there was limited time to complete rigorous academic assignments. As a cohort, we studied together, staying up all night to ensure that assignments were done correctly. Each day, during the two-week residency, it felt like a week of class assignments. We were housed in different parts of the city and decided to use a cohort member's home to work on assignments together.

Staffing changes during the second residency provided new leadership for the program. As a cohort we decided to stay at the same hotel, which provided better study room options and proved to be stress free. Class assignments during the residency were given at the beginning of the summer, allotting us to complete coursework in a timely manner. The second residency began the selection of the dissertation chair and committee members. At this point, the cohort had a full academic year to cultivate relationships with our professors to make informed decisions about who we wanted to serve as our dissertation chair and committee members.

Committee Selection

When selecting the dissertation committee, the program coordinator gave the cohort a list of full-time faculty. Four committee members were required, three committee members from the institution and one faculty member from another institution. Choosing my committee was difficult; meeting with professors to see if they were a good fit for the committee was stressful. Two cohorts were vying for the same professors to chair or sit on committees. After finalizing my committee members, I began the brainstorming process with my chair and committee members. There was a constant transformation of my dissertation topic. We finally agreed, and the research began. Having all of my committee members at the same institution worked well for me. Gathering them to discuss my dissertation process was stress-free. My committee motivated and encouraged me throughout the process toward successful completion.

A graduate student should select a chair who will be supportive and provide guidance through the dissertation-writing process. Also, make sure that the committee members will be collaborative. The committee-selection process is critical to the success in completing the doctoral program. Plus, make certain to have a methodologist on the committee who can help guide his/her colleagues best. Having a great committee will either enhance or weaken one's process. A student should always stay motivated, focused, and determined to reach his/her goal in completing a degree.

Academic and Internship Phase

Balancing both a full-time job and online courses proved to be difficult. Managing time became a priority throughout this doctoral journey. Taking a day each week to step away from the doctoral process will be significant. I felt guilty sometimes. However, I enjoyed the day away from academic rigor and research. The program required two internships that needed to complete before the start of the dissertation phase. The internships were great; this gave me an opportunity to have internships with an organization and a person I wanted to pattern my career after. The internship allowed the cohort to have practical experiences on our path to leadership at the K–12 or higher education levels.

During the academic coursework, I appreciated faculty members who were creative in facilitating their online classes and gave valuable feedback. It is important for professors to be creative while teaching online classes; this provides an invaluable learning experience and adds significance to the students' knowledge. Giving feedback is important for the growth of the student. Moore and Kearsley (2005) suggest that providing significant interaction between the instructor and the student is crucial for successful learning outcomes.

Comprehensive Exams

Comprehensive exams will vary at institutions. The comprehensive exam at Hampton University was an online ten-page paper we had one week to complete. The program provided an online study guide and tutorial for the cohort to study. This was optional for students. I took advantage of the study guide and tutorial and passed the comprehensive exam. Everyone wasn't as fortunate to pass the comprehensive exam, and unfortunately some were dismissed from the program after their second attempt. Because there are varying comprehensive exams at each institution, students should take the exams seriously.

Dissertation Phase

When I was starting my dissertation phase, I wrote at least fifteen minutes a day, which proved to be significant for me. My chair would always tell me that "words on paper" were important. It was a tough journey, writing many iterations of each chapter. After receiving feedback, I usually waited a few hours to look at the critiques. Having a clear mind to assess my critiques proved to strengthen my growth as a student. "Successful completion of the degree depends on the relationship between you and the chair or supervisor of the program" (as cited in Erichsen, Bolliger, & Halupa, 2012, p. 323). Heath (2002) and Manathunga (2005, p. 323) suggest that the "amount of contact that you have with your supervisor results in a successful degree completion." "Regular feedback from your chair is related to degree completion as well as overall student satisfaction with the program" (as cited in Erichsen et al., 2012, p. 323).

The dissertation phase is where one realizes whether one is motivated to conduct the research. It can be a lonely process. Reaching out to other people who have gone through the dissertation process for guidance and support can be valuable. A student should remember that he/she is the subject matter expert. This is a process everyone has to go through, so stay focused and stay humble.

Career Preparedness

Hampton University armored me with the leadership and management skills necessary to work in higher education administration. The institution has provided course curricula and professors that have provided guidance to appreciate great leadership. President Harvey's leadership at Hampton University has motivated me even more to become a college president. Attending his leadership institute for aspiring college presidents is a future goal. The guidance, support, and network I received at Hampton University will impact my career decisions for years to come.

Educational Management Program Students' Perspectives

Hampton University's Educational Management Program students completed a survey discussing their experiences in the online program. Their names were changed for anonymity. The following questions were asked:

1. What made you to decide to attend an online doctoral program at an HBCU?

    Isaiah: I received information about this online doctoral program from listening to the Tom Joyner Show. There was a special pertaining to the HBCU Online Program.
    Karmon: I had attended the university as an undergraduate. The idea of taking classes at home seemed more conducive to my busy schedule
    Patrice: I chose the online modality because I needed flexibility and the ability to be at home with my children. Hampton University (HU) was my first choice for a doctoral program for two reasons: 1. HU is my alma mater; and 2. The Educational Management Program complements my desire to become a university president. It is not general educational administration—it's management.
    Kourtney: It was a new program and because it had been twelve years since I'd completed my master's degree, I thought I would be better suited for a new program.
    Rhonda: I decided to attend an online doctoral program because I felt that at the time it was more convenient for my lifestyle considering

I am a single mother of three. This is a personal goal for me, and I will achieve it no matter what.

2. **What was it like meeting your cohort members, and how did you work with your cohort members throughout the doctoral process?**

    Isaiah: It was interesting finally "putting a face" to each name. Further, it was a very educational experience being exposed to a diversity of thoughts and educational philosophies. Further, it was very beneficial to work with cohorts because we supported each other in completing a myriad of assignments.

    Karmon: I really liked the format of starting the program in summer session, face-to-face. It allowed me to meet my cohort members before starting the online classes and to put faces with names. It also allowed for a bonding period.

    Patrice: I can recall the very first day of our summer residency—everyone stayed to themselves except one guy in particular. This outgoing person brought the cohort together in laughter and conversation. Although the cohort membership declined over time, a core group stayed together as a "family." We e-mailed, texted, telephoned, and even held conference calls during our coursework phase. During the dissertation process, we seemingly went our separate ways—each working at our own pace. I maintain contact with one of my colleagues—although I will always have a special place in my heart and life for all of them. Of the group of four: two finished the program, one is in the finishing stages, and one has encountered setbacks because of family obligations.

    Kourtney: Whereas I was excited about meeting new people, there was some anxiety because many of my cohort members were already connected by sorority affiliation. We worked together as long as we were together and gave earnest effort while apart in our various states for a time. However, we stopped collaborating as a whole group.

    Rhonda: I was excited to meet my cohort members because we were going through this together and it was a support group for us. We worked together on projects, bounced ideas off of each other, and also held conference calls during the course work process and after to see everyone's progress with the dissertation research process.

3. **How was your residency experience in this doctoral program?**

    Isaiah: The residency was a very busy and rigorous experience for two reasons. First, the residency lasted for a period of two weeks. Second, there was a litany of assignments to complete in this short time period.

Karmon: The first residency experience I stayed at home and commuted. The second experience I stated in a local hotel near the campus. The university didn't really offer much housing during the two-week session. Apparently campus housing was available, but that option wasn't clearly conveyed—at least in my opinion. Most of my classmates stayed in the same hotel during the summer residency, so it allowed us to get together and complete group assignments and form study groups.

Patrice: The residency experience was a great way to connect with your colleagues in person. We spent two weeks working closely together commiserating over coursework, laughing over dinner, and helping each other as needed. It was like a homecoming at the second session—which helped to solidify our connections with each other.

Kourtney: During the two required summers on campus, the residency experience was positive.

Rhonda: I enjoyed my residency experience because I not only learned from my course work, but I gained life-long friendships through the process also.

4. How did you balance your academic commitment with personal commitments?

Isaiah: I had to be very organized and "budget" my time to ensure that my assignments were completed efficiently.

Karmon: It was hard to balance the academic commitment with personal commitments. I found I used my weekend time to complete class work, as most assignments were due weekly and usually on Sunday. When I started the program, I was in a committed relationship. That relationship ended a year into the program. My mate didn't understand the time commitment. In addition, I've had to drastically cut down on sorority and family events. I've found it increasingly hard since starting the dissertation phase.

Patrice: Just do it. I do not subscribe to giving or accepting excuses—although at times, things may not go as planned. My academic commitments were secondary to my family and work commitments but were given increased attention when deemed necessary. It was challenging not being able to be as social at times during the holidays because of course work. However, I am used to the consistent demand of time and attention. The balance is fluid—you do what is necessary at the time that it is required.

Kourtney: The first two years I prioritized my academic commitment. When I no longer felt connected to my cohort and the HBCU professors and administrative staff, the commitment weakened.

Rhonda: I balanced my academic commitment and personal commitment by trying to hold myself accountable. I have been keeping a calendar for myself, etc. Now as I am still in my dissertation phase, I can't say it has been easy, but I have to remember the end goal.

5. How was the feedback from your professors, chair, or editor beneficial or challenging throughout your doctoral process?

Isaiah: There have been some deficiencies with the feedback from some professors and chairs in this program. Unfortunately, this program did not employ sufficient full-time professors. As a result, some professors could not commit the necessary time to serve students. However, there were other professors who were very professional in contacting students.

Karmon: Feedback in the program has been challenging. I've experienced losing a chair and miscommunication with other professors with taking over the chairmanship. I very rarely receive feedback from the program chair, as they have switched leadership numerous times without fully sharing with the doctoral students. I think the lack of communication is due to the newness of the program, and I hope it's gotten better with each new cohort.

Patrice: I appreciated every comment, suggestion, wry or congratulatory e-mail, returned or unreturned telephone call, or slap on the hand or back from my professors and chair. The experience was mixed—and certainly, it became what I made of it. From this experience, I learned patience and the practice of it. Being an online instructor myself, however, I expected a lot more from my online instructors and the program coordinators—so I had to temper my expectations with making it through successfully.

Kourtney: While I was on campus, the feedback was phenomenal from my professors. Thereafter, communication declined. I blamed myself because I was made to feel and understand that I "guided the ship." However, I do believe that more communication could have been initiated by my chair. Eventually I expressed my needs with clarity, and my chair at the time obliged. Later I had to select another chair due to career advancement for my original dissertation chairperson.

Rhonda: At the beginning it was not great because I believe the chair I had was overwhelmed with other responsibilities, but now I can say it is much better.

After surveying students in the program, I realized that our journey in the program was similar, validating my experiences in the program. Everyone developed personal and professional relationships and wanted to see the other students succeed. Some students expressed issues communicating with professors and chairs. Changes in program leadership seemed to resolve those issues.

Author's Perception of Best Practices of the Online PhD Program at Hampton University

Hampton University provides a cost-effective, comprehensive online PhD program that fits the needs of full-time working students. The program has seven cohorts and has graduated more than ten students in the last four years. Continuing the tradition of starting the cohorts in the residency phase by utilizing the traditional "face-to-face" models helps to create bonds, friendships, and a family culture among the students. This also fosters relationships with professors. Cohorts have peer mentoring, which creates a support system. Acquiring full-time professors who are creative in their delivery of the online courses lends to the success of the student. The program is incorporating scholarly writing pertaining to the dissertation earlier in the program, guaranteeing completion of the program in a timely manner. Communication of learning outcomes and degree-completion goals has been very effective over the last few years.

Comparing PWIs and HBCUs

Attending two PWIs for my bachelor's and master's degrees makes me appreciate my experience at an HBCU. Although I was a motivated student at both institutions, I did not receive the same welcoming from professors and staff as I encountered at Hampton University.

While attending the PWI for my undergraduate degree, I was the only Black girl in the marching band, the Student Government Association (SGA), and the Student Senate. Many times, in these spaces I did not feel like I belonged. Being the only Black student in class made me feel ostracized at times. I often wondered whether my professors knew my name or if they were concerned about my educational success and career path. Although I was involved in a sorority and other extracurricular activities, I still felt like a number. My institution lacked diverse professors and staff and I was desperate to have relationships with my professors, but it wasn't there. I had a professor and mentor, Dr. Carrie Dunson, who was the only Black professor at the institution at the time. She was the only person that I felt I could talk with about academic concerns or career advice. She helped me navigate the higher education system. Seeing friends drop out for various reasons, mainly because they didn't have guidance and support, was heartbreaking. I had similar experiences receiving my master's degree at a PWI. I desired to have relationship with diverse faculty and staff. However we didn't have many on campus. The student body also lacked diversity; it was difficult to form bonds and relationships with other students. Helping diverse students navigate higher education systems through graduation completion and beyond has always been my mission.

Potential students are sometimes apprehensive about attending an HBCU. Stories that spread about financial aid and housing create anxiety in choosing an institution. My decision to attend an HBCU to obtain a PhD has been the most rewarding decision I have made. Having the "family" culture along with having diverse faculty and staff that care about your educational success and career path have been critical to my success. The nurturing and guidance that I felt was something I yearned for at the PWIs, and I received it at the HBCU. Being a part of a network of Blacks in academia motivates me to do more for my community. I'm elated to be a part of the rich tradition of Hampton University. HBCUs give students the tools necessary to succeed in society, and that is what I appreciate the most.

Advice and Recommendations for Future Graduate Students

Selecting an Institution

When selecting an institution, a student should research the program to ensure that his/her needs are met academically and professionally. Make sure the institution is accredited. If a person decides to work full time, he/she should find an institution that will pair well with his/her work life balance.

Financial Obligations

Selecting an institution that is cost effective is key. At the graduate level, be mindful of how much financial aid (loans) you need for the program. Think about tuition as well as other outside costs, such as traveling, books, materials, graduation robes etc. The cost of books, materials, and other things, such as traveling for residencies, proposal, final defenses, and hotels, can be expensive.

Humble Pie

Throughout the doctoral process a person can become frustrated. However, staying positive with a clear mind are proven strategies that work. Remember, you will be working with people who have different personalities. Stay humble throughout the process; ultimately obtaining the degree is the goal. Everyone at the institution wants you to succeed.

Mentorship

Having mentors is the key to success in all students' future endeavors. After acceptance into Hampton University, I gathered colleagues and friends who have doctoral degrees, to communicate with them about their doctoral process. I also reached out to former and current college presidents, to make sure that I am moving in the right direction with my academic and career goals. Having someone to "bounce" ideas off of is so critical during the doctoral journey. During this process, cultivate and maintain the relationship with mentors by calling, e-mailing, or texting at least once a month. Providing mentors with updates on the doctoral progression goes a long way.

Family and Friends

It will be hard to express how a person feels with family members or friends who have not been through this doctoral process; unfortunately, they do not understand what a doctoral candidate is going through. I learned the hard way. Do not take this personally. Just know that they love and support you. Love them but let them know that you are going through a process that you need to focus on, and ask them for the gift of time. This is the most important thing that a student can do to get through this doctoral journey.

Conclusion

Attending an HBCU online PhD program with a cohort model can be a rewarding experience. Selecting an institution that is cost effective is important. Online PhD programs have grown and have proved to be a successful path to degree completion. Maintaining relationships with the cohort members throughout the dissertation journey is vital. Creative professors, in online class facilitation, who give feedback prove to be very crucial for students' success during the doctoral process. Selecting the dissertation committee is critical. Having guidance and support from professors, chairs, and editors will be beneficial throughout this doctoral process. Motivated students who communicate effectively with professors, chairs, and committee members will have success. Prioritizing the academic coursework with a full-time job is critical. Having tenacity in the program will result in the successful completion of the program.

References

Bista, K., & Cox, D. (2014). Cohort-based doctoral programs, what we have learned over the last 18 years. *The Journal of Doctoral Studies, 9*, 1–20. Retrieved from http://ijds.org/Volume9/IJDSv9p001–020Bista0425.pdf

Erichsen, E. A., Bolliger, D. U., & Halupa, C. (2012). Student satisfaction with graduate supervision in doctoral programs primarily delivered in distance education settings. *Studies in Higher Education, 39*(2), 321–338.

Fuller, J., Risner, M., Lowder, L., Hart, M., & Bachenheimer, B. (2014). Graduates' reflections on an online doctorate in educational technology. *TechTrends, 54*(4), 73–80.

Garrison, D. R., & Arbaugh, J. B. (2007). Researching the community of inquiry framework: Review, issues, and future directions. *Internet and Higher Education, 10*(3), 157–172.

Heath, T. (2002). A quantitative analysis of PhD students' views of supervision. *Higher Education Research and Development, 21*(1), 19–32.

Kumar, S., & Dawson, K. (2012). Theory to practice: Implementation and initial impact of an online doctoral program. *Online Journal of Distance Learning Administration, 15*(1). Retrieved from http://www.westga.edu/~distance/ojdla/spring151/kumar_dawson.html

Manathunga, C. (2005). Early warning signs in postgraduate research education: A different approach to ensuring timely completions. *Teacher in Higher Education, 10*(2), 219–233.

Moore, M., & Kearsley, G. (2005). *Distance education: A systems view* (2nd ed.). Belmont, CA: Wadsworth.

Rausch, D. W., & Crawford, E. K. (2012). Cohort, communities of inquiry, and course delivery methods: UTC best practices in learning-the hybrid learning community model. *The Journal of Continuing Higher Education, 60*(3), 175–180.

9   Twice the Experiences
Graduate School at Two Comprehensive HBCUs

Stevie L. Lawrence II

Minority access to graduate education has captured the concern of admissions officers, professors, and administrators over the last two decades. Johnson-Bailey, Valentine, Cervero, and Bowles (2009) allude to the long and troubled record that Black Americans have had within the American higher education system and more specifically, their plight to receive graduate and professional degrees from colleges and universities across the country. Today, many still debate the importance of Historically Black Colleges and Universities (HBCUs) as viable higher education options for Black students. However, my experiences at an HBCU not only prepared me to succeed academically but also prepared me for my future aspirations. In this chapter I document my experiences at an HBCU for my graduate education and discuss how my institution cultivated my academic ability.

The Undergraduate Experience and Preparing for Graduate School

The level of exposure to the culture of college prior to undergraduate enrollment is uniquely important. This plays a critical role on how far an individual chooses to advance his or her education. For me, that exposure was primarily through participation in Upward Bound, which is a federally funded educational program that came into existence under the Economic Opportunity Act of 1964 and the Higher Education Act of 1965. Participating in this program allows students the ability to more than double their chances of graduating from college.

My experiences as a part of the Upward Bound Math and Science Southeastern Regional Institute at Morehouse College had a significant impact on my college enrollment, persistence, and graduation. Attending this program as a high school sophomore and junior opened the world of higher education up for me. Although the idea of me attending college had been discussed in the home, these early college access experiences made going to college very real.

Undergraduate school at North Carolina Agricultural and Technical State University (NC A&T) was a life changing experience in more ways than one.

As the institution is most often referred to as "A&T," it is steeped in tradition, both academically and socially. Experiences at this institution allowed for lifelong friendships and connections with faculty, staff, and peers. Upon graduation, the university strongly encouraged us to enroll in graduate school. A&T promoted students to strive for graduate education to ensure our career advancement and further development of our skill set to serve the Black community. As a result of attending A&T, I had a strong desire to attend graduate school. Earning a master's degree in public administration was what seemed right, particularly because of my interest to pursue a career in local and state government administration at that time.

Making My Graduate School Selection

Given my desire to earn a master's degree in public administration, I had several options to consider for graduate school. Through my search, Howard University and North Carolina Central University (NCCU) became my top two choices. Ultimately, I selected NCCU for several reasons, which included the cost of attendance because it was a public in-state institution and the fact that it has a liberal arts foundation. This institution has a cadre of masters and professional degree programs, including a renowned School of Law. Placing a critical eye on the number of graduate and professional degree programs that NCCU has, the institution has been actively involved in the education of Blacks at the graduate level for many years. Fountaine (2012) inferred "the role of HBCUs in graduate education has been impressive as they have been a critical force in the productivity of Black graduate and first professional degree recipients" (p. 136).

The history of Black colleges and universities is a unique chapter in the development of American higher education, particularly when one considers the area of graduate education. With this, from a student perspective, the transition from an undergraduate student to a graduate student is significant. Attending undergraduate school at an institution that was heavily focused on STEM was a great experience, but the one down side was that the university did not place emphasis on preparing students for the enjoyment of the liberal arts curriculum. Although the academic departments did provide a great deal of training and preparation for graduate school, like many graduate students nationwide, I experienced difficulty when initially transitioning to graduate school.

Making the Transition as a Graduate Student

Upon arriving at NCCU as a graduate student, there were a number of obstacles that came about. One was the ability to write on the graduate level. Whereas I was a history major and writing was a critical component of my undergraduate education, I unfortunately realized that I was not fully prepared to handle the writing expectations for graduate students. As a result,

I was initially offered to take a professional writing course to hone these skills. I was extremely reluctant to take the course and insisted that I did not need it because I believed my writing skills were adequate. However, through much debate with departmental administration, the course became a requirement. Now reflecting on my experiences, I did in fact need the course, as it proved to be beneficial as I matriculated through my master's program. Interestingly, while I was enrolled in graduate school, some of my peers questioned my decision to attend NCCU.

Before and after enrollment at NCCU, many of my peers would ask, "Why did you decide to attend another Black school?" I would just laugh and reply, "Why not?" From my standpoint, I thought it was important to support these institutions, as they paved the way for Black access to higher education. It bewildered me how many of my peers wanted to detach themselves from such a legacy, believing that these institutions provided a substandard education and that they were somehow second rate. It was important for me to broach to my peers that attending a Black college for graduate school not only provided me with greater success, but it also helped me to acquire the necessary skill set to become competitive in the job market.

According to Nelms (2010), at their best, America's HBCUs have been one of or if not the most productive sectors and the most diverse system of higher education in the world. Much of this can be attributed to their ability to survive many of the challenges they have faced during their conception. It is obvious that these institutions oftentimes suffer from low retention and graduation rates and currently grapple with the need to change their recruiting strategies, which, in turn, provides for a revolving student demographic (Patterson, Dunston, & Daniels, 2013). Therefore, with a changing student demographic, HBCUs are having to implement more innovative methods for retention models even at the graduate level.

Patterson et al. (2013) emphasized the important role that student engagement plays when institutions are attempting to increase student retention rates. Before entering graduate school at NCCU, I was not actively involved in academic-focused activities. At that time, social activities were much more important to me at the undergraduate level. However, unknowingly, NCCU had an institutional tradition, which was deeply rooted in service learning, which allowed for a great deal of student engagement opportunities, even for graduate students. Patterson et al. posited that the term "engagement refers to higher education activities that are simultaneously scholarly and intellectual pursuits that serve the public interest" (p. 158). The graduate program in public administration at NCCU was based solely on service in the public interest, which provided for an increased level of appreciation for the institution's work in a greater context. Moreover, I was able to see NCCU's impact in the community that surrounded the institution. As a graduate student at NCCU, I was able to engage in some of the experiences that I should have taken part of as an undergraduate student.

As a result, NCCU cultivated my hunger to be greater and to leave with a sense of purpose.

The Black college experience at the graduate level provided an extension of the academic empowerment provided by faculty, which I experienced as an undergraduate student. The classroom experiences at A&T were so powerful that I wanted to experience it again and again. It became a drug of sorts, and I was seriously addicted to it. In my case, I observed faculty as not only my teachers but as my parents away from home who had a specific responsibility to ensure I was successful. As a result, I achieved not only for my individual success but to show my professors that their support and advice were being applied.

The literature surrounding the level of connectedness between Black students and Black faculty at HBCUs suggests that this relationship has a tremendous impact on how Black students persist toward graduation at HBCUs. Rucker and Gendrin (2003) noted this as teacher immediacy, where teachers and students develop a perception of physical or psychological closeness. Moreover, Rucker and Gendrin found that Black students had stronger support in classes taught by Black instructors. In particular, the students believed that their Black instructors were more nurturing and welcoming than their White counterparts. With regard to Rucker and Gendrin's research, their findings are parallel to my experiences as a graduate student at NCCU.

Graduate school at NCCU challenged me in ways that I could have never imagined. Being in an environment with so many like-minded individuals pushed me to become serious about academics. Enrolling in graduate school provided me the opportunity to participate in a number of professional development opportunities, which had an underlying theme related to service learning and student engagement. Among them was the chance to serve as a Public Alley, which is a national public service program. I interned with the Hayti Heritage Center, serving as its marketing and program coordinator. This opportunity gave me the chance to interact with persons from all walks of life, in an effort to market the center's cultural arts programs to the surrounding community. This was truly the starting point for my career. Following this opportunity, through the institution's commitment to public service, I was given another opportunity to serve as the HBCU campus outreach coordinator with Common Cause North Carolina, promoting civic engagement at three HBCUs in North Carolina, namely NCCU, A&T, and Fayetteville State University. These professional development opportunities truly prepared me for what I was going to encounter later in my career.

It was during my tenure at NCCU, serving as the HBCU Campus Outreach Coordinator, that I had the epiphany to embark on a career in higher education. Much of this I believe was in part due to my overall experiences in college, and through divine intervention from God, as this work seems to be a field in which an individual must be called or appointed to do by some higher source, just as professional minister in the Christian faith.

Using My Faith as Motivator

For me, the journey to earning a master's degree became very spiritual. There were all sorts of forces that pulled me. I oftentimes felt isolated, as if others really did not truly understand my reasoning to pursue a higher level of education. In addition, at points throughout my matriculation at NCCU, I felt that the curriculum was too challenging. Before enrollment, I assessed the program, and in my analysis, I believed the program would surely be quite easily completed. This was certainly an underestimation of the curriculum and the program's faculty. Graduate school required a higher level of thinking. Furthermore, it required well-developed analytical and writing skills in order to be successful. Therefore, I found that the writing course I was recommended was certainly needed. Considering all these obstacles, there was a heavy reliance of my faith in God, reinforced by the program's director of student services, Mrs. Rosa Anderson.

I have vivid memories of the numerous conversations she and I would have concerning my matriculation. She continuously encouraged me to use God as my source of strength to be successful. Although she was not actually a faculty member, she was so instrumental in my holistic development, and our relationship remains very strong to this day. Her interaction with me will always be cherished, as her advice was just as valuable as faculty members of the program, if not more in some regards based on our connection spiritually. Flowers, Scott, Riley, and Palmer (2015) emphasized the importance of faculty and student interaction and the impact it has on students' satisfaction with the college experience. Clearly, I was motivated by the caring and supportive staff at NCCU.

NCCU Preparing Me for the Future

Looking back on my experience at NCCU, it goes without question that this institution prepared me professionally. It was there that the skills that are necessary for survival in the professional world were developed. Considering the great role that NCCU played in my development, my experience there was different compared to my experience at A&T. Coming from an environment like A&T, I expected everything to be the same from a student perspective, especially because it was an HBCU. The perception was that the culture at all Black schools was the same. It became evident that this was not necessarily true, and it didn't take long for me to determine that. There were drastic differences in the ways in which students expressed their love for NCCU. I always explain to prospective students when trying to determine between these two institutions, whether at the undergraduate or graduate level, that they should first make sure the institution meets their academic needs, but institutional compatibility is significantly important to student retention. Students must take in account their personalities and determine if they fit the institutional landscape.

Students at NCCU were much more reserved in terms of displaying their pride for the institution. I was accustomed to a much more direct, and at times, blatant expression of school pride. NCCU has a very rich legacy, but its traditions are much different from their rival institution, A&T. Not everything required such pomp and circumstance as it did at A&T; this was something I had to become used to. However, NCCU did have its appeal, as the atmosphere seemed to be a little more inclusive. This simply means that the institution is smaller, and at times, they were able to provide a little more attention to some areas for me personally. I did really enjoy that about the institution. I made it my business to really get to know people around campus, even more so than I did as an undergraduate student.

Graduating from NCCU was a tremendous accomplishment for me. I was the first person from my high school class to earn a graduate degree, only the second in my family to do so. Therefore, it was a big deal. I remember the graduation ceremony distinctly. I was very emotional; everyone continued to ask why, but I could not really explain exactly why I was. I just knew that I had completed something that would benefit me for many years to come. I had become so connected to those who assisted in my matriculation, and to witness it come to fruition was worth every situation that presented itself as a barrier for me. As I sat there ready to have my degree conferred, my mind rolled back to that "one-stop shop" I had attended at Guilford Community College in order to enroll at NCCU.

Looking to the Future: Deciding to Earn My PhD

Upon completing my graduate degree at NCCU, I knew that earning a doctoral degree was something I wanted to accomplish. Immediately after graduate school at NCCU, obtaining a position in higher education was very important. Ultimately, I was able to begin professional work as the associate director and learning coach for an African American Male Achievement Program at a community college in Northeastern North Carolina. It was there that I knew I wanted to pursue a doctoral degree in higher education.

After determining that this was the route I wanted to pursue, making a decision about where to obtain a doctoral degree was a significant piece of the puzzle. Earning yet another degree from an HBCU was the appropriate option for me. Even with this notion, a major part of me understood that oftentimes employers look for diversity in the institutions where prospective employees receive their professional training. It was without question that I would receive the academic and personal support from faculty at an HBCU during the process of completing my terminal degree. I applied to a number of institutions. Among them were the University of Pennsylvania, North Carolina State University, Hampton University, North Carolina A&T State University, Morgan State University, and Jackson State University.

There were a number of issues that contributed to making my final decision, one of which was how accommodating the chosen degree program was for a working adult, as I desired to continue gaining professional experience in higher education while pursuing my graduate degree. Initially, I was very interested in attending Hampton University and earning a PhD in educational management. However, I became very interested in Jackson State's University's (JSU) Executive PhD Program in urban higher education after researching the availability of doctoral degree programs in higher education at HBCUs. Although there were some initial thoughts about attending a predominantly White institution for my terminal degree, I knew what would be the perfect fit for me.

Personally, I needed to feel what I felt in the classroom at A&T and NCCU just once more. I knew that this would be the finale. Furthermore, I wanted to experience higher education in a different form. This meant pursuing a degree at an institution that was outside the norm among my peers as well as my colleagues in higher education. The HBCUs in the university system of North Carolina were familiar to me, and I wanted something different, but with another "flavor" of sorts to it. I understood that there would be differences from what I had already been experienced. As stated, higher education had become like an addiction to me. At this point I could not get enough.

The enrollment process for JSU was very extensive. There were many pieces associated with the application, and I wanted to submit the very best application packet possible. I distinctly remember reading the instructions, which emphasized that the Executive PhD Program looked very favorably on applications that included letters of reference from college presidents. I was very strategic; I solicited the support of one of my mentors, Dr. Ervin V. Griffin Sr., a very experienced community college president, along with Dr. Claude G. Perkins, the president of Virginia Union University, where I was working during the time of the application process. I obtained these, along with a letter of then vice president for academic affairs, Dr. W. Franklin Evans, who has gone on to serve as the interim president at South Carolina State University. I had all the right pieces in place. Finally, the submission deadline was approaching, and I completed and submitted the application packet. Several weeks later I was informed of an opportunity to interview over the phone with the admissions panel, which I did. I knew that I had conducted a stellar interview. The waiting time between that point and being informed of acceptance and denial seemed like an eternity. I literally could not eat, sleep, or function. All I was able to do was go to work.

The process almost consumed me, as this was so important to me. I had become very anxious about learning if I was accepted. Although I had applied to other institutions, my number one choice was JSU. That is what I wanted; there was something about the program, and my heart did not desire anything else. During the process for applying to doctoral programs, I had confided in several colleagues about my intentions. One in particular was the director of career services at Virginia Union University. One morning, she passed me in the student center and asked if I had gotten a response from any of the doctoral programs. I indicated that I had not and that I had become very anxious. She followed by quoting a Bible verse that states, "Be anxious for nothing, but in everything by prayer and supplication, with thanksgiving, let your requests be made known to God, and the peace of God, which surpasses all understanding, will guard your hearts and minds through Christ Jesus" (Philippians 4:6–7, English Standard Version).

I took what she told me and walked back to my office; it was then I discovered an e-mail indicating that I had been accepted to pursue my PhD in higher education at JSU. I was extremely overjoyed. What a coincidence this was. That is when I knew that fate had led me to the right program for this final degree I was seeking. The experience at JSU was all that I expected it to be and more. Everything during the enrollment process was near perfect. It reminded me tremendously of A&T; I felt right at home.

What really attracted me to enroll at this particular institution for my doctoral degree was knowing that the faculty in the program were very experienced. Seeking to become a college administrator, I believe that much knowledge can be acquired from the theoretical concepts of leadership in education and understanding the nuances associated with college student development. However, I truly believe that with theory there must be a balance, which is learning through demonstration, application, and practice.

This was exactly what the Executive PhD Program at JSU allowed for. During the time of enrollment, I was very focused on my career endeavors. The first two degrees I earned were not sought solely for a purpose of career advancement. This time around I was confident about how earning this particular degree would have a positive impact on my professional career. Being taught by faculty who had been exactly where I was attempting to go in my career was what made JSU's program seem "full of life." Reading and researching what this doctoral program had to offer, it did not seem as if it was a mere collection of classes providing for a course of study that might not actually be applicable to field of higher education.

I knew that being admitted to this doctoral program would allow me the opportunity to be taught and mentored by some of the best, who had worked in the trenches, saving and preserving the legacy of HBCUs. There were individuals who had or currently served in such roles as president and vice president at HBCUs all across the country. JSU was certainly not what I had expected. Not that I expected anything less than I experienced. This could have been because program has a great amount of visibility at the institution. It seemed as if the entire institution knew who was enrolled in the program, and they congratulated them with much enthusiasm. The campus community also seemed eager to assist with their matriculation in any way that they could.

Not being from Mississippi, I really did not understand what JSU was and what it actually meant to the people from this area of the country, in terms of its influence and how it was viewed from a variety of stakeholders. This institution is literally the hallmark of higher education for Black Mississippians and one of the premier institutions in the Deep South, which has provided access and equity to higher education for Blacks for many generations.

As my enrollment at JSU was much more strategic and concentrated, so was the process for instruction and student learning for this specific degree program. As a result, enrollment in my particular doctoral program called for the inclusion and full commitment to the cohort learning model. Participation in such a learning model was something I had never been involved in before. In hindsight, this was certainly the most appropriate method of instruction for me at this time for many reasons. One in particular is the enhancement of skills acquired in team-building activities, which are essential for developing college administrators like myself. Furthermore, after graduating from this program, I totally understand that the program delivery method was certainly created intentionally, as those who seek administrative positions in higher education must be able to successfully maneuver through the academy, with the ability to handle multiple personalities in an effort to accomplish goals, objectives, and priorities.

My cohort included many from varied backgrounds. Oftentimes the HBCU experience is not fully credited for the diversity that it offers. However, the PhD program at JSU offered a tremendous amount of diversity, with consideration given to both students and the program faculty. There was a reasonable amount of Caucasian students and faculty who saw a great deal of value in this particular graduate program. These individuals brought a great amount of energy to the environment.

After the first class session at JSU, there was a particular professor who stood out to me. For some reason, I have always been drawn to teachers who possessed motherly characteristics or provided more than just instruction for students. There was a professor who immediately captured my attention, possessing these very characteristics. As academic advisors were being assigned to our cohort, I hoped that she would be mine. My prayers were answered. After being assigned, I came to learn that her name was Dr. Neari Warner, and she had served as acting president of Grambling State University from 2001 to 2004, during a turbulent period in the institution's history, as its accreditation was being threatened.

I thought to myself, *This is exactly who I need*. I knew she would be able to provide a level of insight and support to me that would be second to none. I did not know that what I was about to encounter with her as my advisor, and ultimately my dissertation chair, would be not only an academic development experience, but it would develop me further personally and spiritually. Initially there were not any reservations about the classes included as a part of the curriculum. With it being multidiscipline in nature, I had been exposed to a majority of the courses, with the exclusion of the courses focused in areas of higher education and student development. The major worry for me, as it is with most doctoral students, was the dissertation process. However, for whatever reason, I had a certain level of comfort within, as I totally believed that everything was going to be just fine. Obtaining this degree would be much different, as I was required to travel for monthly class sessions. Not being directly apart of the day-to-day campus environment required a high level of commitment to accomplish the necessary work.

Being Supported Through the Dissertation Phase

My experience at JSU was phenomenal, but I did not really understand how committed I had to be to the process. As an out-of-state student, I traveled by flight a total of twenty-six times from Raleigh, North Carolina, to Jackson, Mississippi. This was a grueling process, but I knew it would be well worth it in the end. I became such a frequent flyer that the airport personnel came to know me personally, and when they saw me, they knew I was on my way to class at JSU. This was particularly true for those at the airport in Jackson, as it is very small. My experience with my advisor was so intrusive that we often rode on the same flights and traveled to and from campus together, discussing my dissertation topic, which was "Factors That Influence Alumni Giving at Two Historically Black Universities in North Carolina."

She assured me that the topic was timely and was certainly worth merit. She was exactly right. She ensured I had everything I needed and never failed to provide the extra push to ensure I was giving 150 percent to produce a sound scholarly document that would provide for a number of scholarly articles to contribute to the greater body of knowledge surrounding this topic. Her insight could not be matched. She, along with other faculty members who were a part of my matriculation, were committed to my success as a student. Many could not determine quite how I could earn a doctoral degree in twenty-four months, but as a part of the process, students begin to work on their dissertations immediately, transfer twelve credit hours into the program, and enroll in ten credit hours four six consecutive semesters.

Dr. Warner continued to lecture her advisees about how quickly the program would pass, indicating that we did not have time to procrastinate, and time was of the essence. It was through her that I understood completely why JSU was my first choice. The institution provided everything that I need to be successful. I experienced what I was seeking for a second time as a graduate student at JSU. Even as a doctoral student during the first year of the program at twenty-nine years old, I continued to develop strong connections with those who learned beside me. By the conclusion of the program at thirty-one, I had gained an entirely new family. I was a part of something that had a network all across the country. From my viewpoint, there was a distinctive brand associated with earning a doctorate from the Executive PhD Program in urban higher education at JSU.

Earning My PhD and Closing Remarks

On December 12, 2014, I earned my doctorate from JSU. This literally brought my graduate school experiences full circle. All in all, my HBCU graduate school experiences at NCCU and JSU were phenomenal. There is nothing I would change about it. I believe that both of these institutions are examples of pillars of strength in Black graduate education. Each of these universities embodies the core characteristics of pursuing an education from the Black college context, which includes not only providing nurturing environment for students but also ensuring that the curriculum challenges the students not solely academically but holistically. The investments made in these institutions are invaluable. There is not a monetary value that could be placed on what was given to me, as the value is evident in how I have been able to acquire positions related directly to the programs of study. The lessons learned at both institutions will be a part of me forever. Today, I find myself acting as an unofficial recruiter for both institutions.

I have been responsible for many students enrolling in the graduate program in public administration since I graduated. Some have been my own family members. Since graduating from JSU, I have begun to do the same with professionals in higher education who are seeking career advancement. Both of these institutions provided me with an experience so powerful that I want others to feel what I felt. Both of these academic opportunities were life changing. Through pursing graduate school at both of these institutions, and considering their impact on my professional accomplishments to date, I believe that this is a testament to the quality of instruction provided at the graduate level at our nation's HBCUs. Graduate school at both of these institutions was certainly an experience like none other. It was twice the experience.

References

Flowers, A., Scott, J., Riley, J., & Palmer, R. T. (2015). Beyond the call of duty: Building on othermothering for improving outcomes at historically Black colleges and universities. *Journal of African American Males in Education, 6*(1), 59–73.

Fountaine, T. P. (2012). The impact of faculty-student interaction on Black doctoral students attending historically Black institutions. *The Journal of Negro Education, 81*(2), 136–147.

Johnson-Bailey, J., Valentine, T., Cervero, R. M., & Bowles, T. A. (2009). Rooted in soil: The social experiences of Black graduate students at a southern research university. *Journal of Higher Education, 80*(2), 178–203.

Nelms, C. (2010). HBCU reconstruction. *Presidency, 3*(1), 14–19.

Patterson, G., Dunston, Y., & Daniels, K. (2013). Extreme makeover: Preserving the HBCU mission through service learning pedagogy. *Journal of African American Studies, 17*(2), 154–161.

Rucker, M., & Gendrin, D. (2003). The impact of ethnic identification on student learning in the HBCU classroom. *Journal of Instructional Psychology, 30*(3), 207–215.

10 The Significant Value of Historically Black Colleges and Universities

Tara D. Miller

When you do something, do it so well that no man living, or yet to be born can do it better.
—Dr. Benjamin E. Mays, Former Morehouse College, President 1940–1967

The quote written by Dr. Benjamin E. Mays serves as a form of medicated balm, which heals the mental afflictions some Black students encountered during their tenure at an Historically Black College and University (HBCU). Frequently, HBCU graduates or students recount comments from non-HBCU alumni regarding their purpose, "Why are you attending an HBCU when you can enroll at a predominantly White institution (PWI) and receive a quality education?" The statement is troublesome because there are a plethora of successful HBCU graduates. HBCUs continue to enroll graduate and professional students from PWIs and other minority-serving institutions (MSIs) that excel because of the supportive environment they provide.

Some scholars argue that administrators and faculty at HBCUs help students develop vital skills including self-reliance and fortitude. The campus community takes time to nurture students' minds and spirits to combat economic and social barriers. Historically Black Colleges and Universities are institutions that have remained beacons of hope for scholars with dreams, and aspirations of becoming successful. The beauty of HBCUs is that they are a part of America because of philanthropists and pioneers who financed, and built the institutions. The funders welcomed poor newly freed slaves. They realized that providing students with an opportunity to earn a quality education was critical.

False Accusation About HBCUs

Unfortunately, some critics have questioned the relevancy of HBCUs. However, "If it were not for HBCUs, Black Americans from low- and moderate-income backgrounds would not have succeeded." The quote reflects my experience as a graduate student at an HBCU. I received my graduate degree from Florida

Agricultural and Mechanical University (FAMU). I chose to pursue my master's degree in secondary English education at FAMU because I was offered a full scholarship.

Throughout my tenure at FAMU I received a scholarship and $2,500 to write a master's thesis, titled, "The Disinherited and Dispossessed Negroes in Hollywood Films during the 1940s–1990s." In addition, I decided to continue my graduate studies at FAMU because Dr. Frederick S. Humphries, former president of FAMU and Tennessee State University (TSU), was a great motivator and mentor.

While working on my master's degree, I envisioned a time when I would become president of Florida A&M University. During my presidency I would hire the best faculty and help the student body shape their dreams into reality while they earned their bachelors, masters, and doctorates in chemical, electrical, civil, and mechanical engineering, pharmaceutical, zoology, law, mathematics, art history, broadcast journalism, graphic arts, chemistry, and nursing, just to list a few majors. Dr. Humphries's elegant speeches and engagement influenced my decision to continue my education.

Also, the faculty's unrelenting support, love, respect, and encouragement were blessings in my life while I was a graduate student at FAMU. I have never witnessed an associate professor who had a willingness to go with a student to Strozier's Library at Florida State University (FSU) until I met Dr. Virden Evans, my master thesis advisor. Dr. Evans took the time out of his busy schedule to travel with me from Florida A&M University to Florida State University, which is located in Tallahassee.

When I earned my master's degree in secondary English education in 1997, it was one of the happiest days of my life. I felt a sense of accomplishment; my parents, James and Lillie Miller, were elated, and other family members as well. However, my academic journey was not smooth and easy. In fact, it was rigorous, demanding, but rewarding. Earning my master's degree within a year (1996–1997) required prayer, intensive studying, writing papers, revisional writing, researching, note taking, developing a rapport with my professors, collaborative learning, independent studies, mediation, and determination.

Collaborating with classmates with similar experiences, including staying awake to complete research papers, studying for exams, oral presentations, and conducting research on a weekly basis, helped to establish a camaraderie. I developed relationships with individuals with similar goals and believe that led to my success. I interacted with some of the best professors in the world during my time at FAMU, including: Drs. Virden and Adeline Evans, Dr. Fritzrold, Professor Felicia Jones, Professor Howard Williams, Dr. James Hawkins, Dr. Willie T. Williams, Dr. Beulah Hemmingway, Dr. Emma Dawson, and numerous of other professors who supported emerging scholars. Also, Florida A & M University's Graduate School administrators provided scholars with the opportunity to be a part of their Feeder Program. The Graduate Feeder Scholar Program (GFSP), located in the School of Graduate Studies, is an official partnership agreement arranged by FAMU with more than forty participating universities located throughout the United States. Students selected for the GFSP benefitted from working with scholars with similar research interests from a variety of postsecondary institutions.

Doctoral Studies

The FAMU Feeder Program was designed to partner administrators, faculty, and staff with scholars with a 3.00 or higher GPA. Students would have the opportunity to pursue masters, law, doctorate, or medical degrees. The goal of the Feeder Program was to promote graduate education, scholarship, and research among minority students. I benefited from the FAMU Feeder Program because I was offered a full scholarship to Howard University in 1998 to pursue a doctorate in mass communications.

At that time, there was a new department chair, Bill Dukes, an actor and director of the film *Not Easily Broken*, but I declined the offer from Howard University. I decided to attend Clark Atlanta University (CAU) to earn a doctorate in humanities with a concentration in Africana Women's Studies, which required forty-eight hours of course work and twelve hours for the dissertation.

Fortunately the faculty at FAMU prepared me for the rigors of a doctoral program. While I was at FAMU, the faculty placed a strong emphasis on research and writing. When I arrived at CAU, I was responsible for completing forty-eight hours of course work in the Humanities/Africana Women's Studies Program. Students were required to read at least six texts in preparation for each course. Professors required students to write research papers every week that were eighteen to twenty pages in length. After I completed my course requirements, my academic advisor, Dr. Mary Twinning, indicated that I had to prepare for my comprehensive exams. Prior to me taking my comprehensive exams, Dr. Twinning asserted, "Ms. Miller, you only have two opportunities to pass your comprehensive exams. Therefore, you must do your best to pass the first time." I took heed to Dr. Twinning's advice. I passed the comprehensive exams the first time, but I was not finished with the testing requirements. Not only did I have to write questions that were presented in essay format, but I also had to defend my written essay responses in an oral defense before a committee of seven professors in a conference room at Clark Atlanta University.

Awkward Academic Experience

During the oral defense, I thought I was going to collapse because I was fearful that my professors would pose questions I could not answer. Nevertheless, my F.E.A.R. was False Evidence Appearing Real; my professors asked me questions based on the questions I responded to on my comprehensive exams. There were a few questions that I answered that were not on the exam but were related to my discipline.

When I was a graduate student at FAMU, I had to defend my master's thesis. Thus, I had some insight on how to respond during an oral defense. Shortly after my oral defense, I received a response from my academic advisor that I had successfully defended. Fortunately, I moved to the next stage of my academic journey, which was to continue to write and develop my dissertation titled, "Significance of Sexual Representation of African-Americans in Blaxploitation Films: 1970–1974." Before I took the comprehensive exam, one of my former professors, Dr. Josephine Bradley, told me to write a concept paper that could be developed into my dissertation. The advice helped me develop my theoretical framework. The concept paper served as the blueprint for my research.

Reflecting of the Academic Journey and HBCU Critics

After reflecting on my academic journey, my accomplishments would not have been possible without visiting a college as a high school student. When I was sixteen, I had the opportunity to visit a college during the winter break. After arriving on the campus, I was intrigued by the beautifully painted Greek fraternities and sororities' (Delta Sigma Theta's, Alpha Phi Alpha's, and Omega Phi Psi's) images on the walls of the university. The landscape, well-manicured lawn and hedges, and immaculate campus view convinced me to attend the university. Whereas I believe HBCUs are "diamonds in the rough," there are some critics who believe they are no longer relevant.

For example, two faculty members at a PWI wrote a derogatory editorial, which bashed the presidents, faculty, and students from HBCUs. The authors asserted, "Black colleges are academic disaster areas, and an ill financed, ill-staffed caricature of white higher education" (Jencks & Riesman, 1968, p. 324). The assumption that HBCUs are incapable of providing Black students with a quality education reinforces racial stereotypes. The comments suggested HBCUs are mimicking PWIs and don't have a history of success. However, HBCUs provide Black students from low- and moderate-income backgrounds with a curriculum that recognizes the contributions of ethnic and racial groups

Dr. Joseph Baldwin, in an article titled, "Notes on an Afrocentric Theory of Black Personality," wrote about the European cosmology. Specifically, he indicated:

> In European cosmology the so-called human-nature relations are separated, compartmentalized, and independent. One could say that a basic emphasis in the European reality structure is toward "exclusiveness."

The basic theme characterizing European cosmology is that of "man versus man or nature," of conflict and antagonism, with the emphasis being on man's mastery and control over other humans or nature through domination, oppression, suppression and unnatural alteration.
(1981, p. 173)

The statement suggests that Jencks and Riesman's distorted thinking reinforces stereotypes based on race. According to Dr. Baldwin, "African-Americans are led by an African cosmology, which is characterized by 'Man-Nature Harmony' or Unity, oneness of being" (p. 171). Throughout my academic career administrators, faculty, and staff provided a nurturing environment. Jencks and Riesman's assumption is inconsistent with HBCUs' history of educating a cadre of scholars in law, literature, and political science.

Unfortunately, Jencks and Riesman are not alone in their thinking. Critics including Michael Meyers contended, "no matter what else is taught, or how well it is taught, the fact that a school is segregated teaches that there is a qualitative difference between students in Black and [in] White colleges" (Willie, 1979, p. 46). Fortunately, I don't regret my decision to attend an HBCU.

Reflecting on a Journey Not Traveled

I am a proud graduate of Florida A&M University with a bachelor's of science degree in broadcast journalism in 1996 and master's of science degree in English in 1997. My success at FAMU continued at Clark Atlanta University, where I completed my doctorate. Choosing between Howard and Clark Atlanta was a difficult decision.

Realization About Howard University

In 1998 I did not recognize Howard University's rich history. The institution was named after the commissioner of the Freedmen's Bureau, General Oliver O. Howard. In retrospect, I would have chosen Howard over Clark Atlanta. Nevertheless, CAU's professors helped prepare me for my future success.

Attending an historically Black college or university allows women and men to flourish as scholars. For instance, after graduating from Florida A&M University and Clark Atlanta, I had the honor to publish textual writings, present papers at various conferences/symposiums, teach at the collegiate-levels at institutions (such as Morehouse College, Spelman College, Clark Atlanta University, Strayer University, DeVry University, Benedict College, Georgia Perimeter College, Tallahassee Community College, University of Phoenix, and Morris Brown College), and to meet President Barack Obama at Morehouse College when he was the commencement speaker in the spring of 2013.

List of Historically Black Colleges and Universities

HBCUs have a long and distinguished history educating Black students. There are a variety of private and public HBCUs located throughout the nation, including the following:

Table 10.1 List of Historically Black Colleges and Universities

Alabama A&M University	Harris-Stowe State University	Norfolk State University	Texas Southern	HBCU
Alabama State University	Hinds Community College	Oakwood University	Tougaloo College	HBCU
Alcorn University	Howard University	Pain College	Tuskegee University	HBCU
Allen University	Howard University School of Law	Paul Quinn College	University of Arkansas at Pine Bluff	HBCU
Arkansas Baptist College	Howard University School of Medicine	Philander Smith College	University of Maryland, Eastern Shore	HBCU
Bethune Cookman University	Interdenominational Theological Center	Prairie View A&M University	University of the Virgin Islands	HBCU
Bennett College	Jackson State	Rust College	University of the Virgin Islands-Kingshill	HBCU
Bishop State Community College	Jarvis Christian College	Savannah State University	Virginia State University	HBCU
Bowie State University	Johnson C. Smith University	Selma University	Virginia Union University	HBCU
Central State University	Kentucky State University	Shaw University	Virginia University of Lynchburg	HBCU
Charles Drew University School of Medicine and Science	Knoxville College Lane College	Shelton State Community College	Voorhees College	HBCU

(Continued)

Table 10.1 (Continued)

Coppin State University	Langston University	Shorter College	West Virginia State University	HBCU
Claflin University	LeMoyne-Owen College	Simmons College of Kentucky	Wilberforce University	HBCU
Clark Atlanta University	Livingstone College	South Carolina State University	Wiley College	HBCU
Delaware State University	Meharry Medical College	Southern University and A&M College	Winston Salem State University	HBCU
Denmark Technical College	Mississippi Valley State University	Southern University at New Orleans	Xavier University	HBCU
Dillard University	Morgan State University	Southwestern Christian College	HBCU	HBCU
Edward Waters College	Morehouse College	Spelman College	HBCU	HBCU
Fisk University	Morehouse School of Medicine	St. Augustine's College	HBCU	HBCU
Florida A&M University	Morris Brown College	St Phillip College	HBCU	HBCU
Florida Memorial University	Norfolk State University	Stillman College	HBCU	HBCU
Gambling State University	North Carolina A&T State University	Talladega College	HBCU	HBCU
Gadsden State Community College	North Carolina Central University	Tennessee State University	HBCU	HBCU
Hampton University	North Carolina Central University School of Law	Texas College	HBCU	

Professors' Advice and the Influence of Dr. Robert Franklin, Former Morehouse President

Professors at HBCUs encourage students to be competitive, focused, and prepared to compete with scholars from other postsecondary institutions. There is a misconception that HBCU professors and students are not quality scholars. However, as a product of two HBCUs, I can attest to their competitive environment. Throughout my doctoral program I worked full-time at Morehouse College and part-time at Clark Atlanta University, where I taught English composition, world literature, reading comprehension, African American literature, and the aesthetic of films.

Teaching students at Morehouse College and Clark Atlanta was a rewarding experience. I served as an instructor and had the opportunity to meet former President of Morehouse College, Dr. Robert Franklin. Dr. Franklin truly inspired the students, the faculty, and me with his great oratorical skills. Dr. Franklin believed that male scholars should epitomize what it means to be a Morehouse man, including traveling and contributing to academia. Dr. Franklin suggested that a Morehouse man should be "well read." He believed that all Morehouse men should communicate effectively. Dr. Franklin contended that reading various literary genres would help to increase a student's vocabulary, insight, and knowledge base. In addition, Dr. Franklin encouraged students to read books, not just summaries of texts, and choose an accomplished and prolific writer as a role model. He says, "books open doors and allows them to peek around the walls that society can sometimes build in front of us" (para. 1). While this is likely the advice that most institutions give to their students and emerging scholars, Morehouse provides an environment that allows Black males to excel.

Dr. Franklin believed that students at Morehouse College should be "well spoken." He understood that Morehouse students had to be articulate to overcome stereotypes regarding Black men. Dr. Franklin suggested, "Good communication reduces the necessity of relying on profanity or empty verbal placeholders like, 'um, uh, ahh, you know, and like' or nonsense like 'you know what I'm saying'" (para. 2). Because of his background as a change agent, Dr. Franklin understood his job included developing a new generation of Black leaders. "Leaders mean what they say, and they say what they mean" (para. 2). One of the greatest leaders from Morehouse College was Rev. Dr. Martin Luther King Jr., a prolific writer, scholar, orator, and humanitarian. Morehouse College is an institution that prides itself on transforming "boys into men." However, Dr. King cannot accept all the credit for his great oratory skills without giving tribute to his father, Martin Luther King Sr., the former pastor at Ebenezer Baptist Church, orator, and graduate of Morehouse College, along with Dr. Benjamin E. Mays, a motivator, orator, mentor, and former president of Morehouse College and graduate.

Dr. Franklin encouraged students to be well traveled. Travel allows people to see how various cultures strive and survive globally. Traveling to various countries reduces bias. Dr. Franklin "encouraged Morehouse's students to go out in the world and break new ground, and to take others with them to improve life for all humanity" (para. 3). Furthermore, Dr. Franklin also espoused the importance of dressing well. Wearing the appropriate attire is very important in a professional or social setting. A well-dressed person depicts confidence. Dr. Franklin continued, "Morehouse does not have a strict dress code, but while the students are there, they will not sag their pants, but because they're there on the ground where Benjamin E. Mays (Morehouse's former president), Martin Luther King Jr. (civil rights activist), and Maynard Jackson (former mayor of Atlanta) walked. They will be well-dressed" (para. 4). Again, a well-dressed person demonstrates he/she has pride in his/her appearance, a quality that separates him/her from other students. Students at the majority of HBCUs will benefit from a nurturing environment where they are encouraged to strive for success.

Last, Dr. Franklin emphasized "balance." Dr. Franklin's philosophy on "balance" mimics five of the army's core values that are taught to soldiers: courage, loyalty, integrity, discipline, and honor. He asserts, "I want the students to be spiritually disciplined, intellectually astute, and morally wise . . . humble and willing to lift others as they climb to new height. Being well-balanced prepares us for the unexpected and allows them the ability to act and react to the world in a positive way" (para. 5). Dr. Franklin's teachings "ensure Morehouse students have the traits to succeed in the global economy." During my tenure at Morehouse College as an instructor, I observed that students from underserved communities benefited from a structured environment. They learn how to become great leaders by adopting Dr. Franklin's teachings.

Surprisingly, not many people realize that Morehouse College was created as a single-gender school because, "White southerners considered efforts by Black people to learn absurd" (Hine, Hine, & Harrold, 2010, p. 274). Therefore, Morehouse College represents the "core of success" because during the 1860s, most Whites threatened to lynch teachers if they taught Blacks, and they burned some schools to the ground.

Henry L. Morehouse, an American Baptist Home Missionary for whom Morehouse College is named, believed the "purpose of education was to develop strong minds." He said, "Gifted intellectuals could lead people forward" (p. 347). Henry L. Morehouse, Dr. Robert M. Franklin, Dr. Frederick S. Humphries, Dr. Tara D. Miller, Dr. Benjamin E. Mays, and many advocates of HBCUs share a similar belief system that the "Men of Morehouse" and graduates of HBCUs can be leaders today and tomorrow. Therefore, I would advise any person who wants to earn a master's or doctoral degree to pursue it at an Historically Black College because he/she will earn a degree that require rigorous studying, thorough research, scholarship, and confidence.

Critical and Stellar Graduates of HBCUs

In spite of people like Jordan Winthrop, who once said, "The Negro species is born as Inferior" (1977, p.135), I would say his statement is a misnomer, which lacks credibility. For example, Historically Black College and University professors have taught students including Thurgood Marshall, the renowned attorney who won the *Brown vs. Broad of Education* case and who was a graduate of Howard University's Law School; W.E.B. Du Bois, the author of the *Souls of Black Folks* and a creator of the *Crisis Magazine;* Terrance J., an *Entertainment Tonight* news host and actor and a graduate of North Carolina A&T University; Oprah Winfrey, one of the most influential journalists nationally and a graduate of Tennessee State University; Debbie Allen and Phylicia Rashad, who both graduated from Howard University; Keisha Knight-Pulliam, who graduated from Spelman College; and Dr. Martin Luther King Jr., scholar, pastor, teacher, author, and advocate for justice, who graduated from Morehouse College. This list of accomplished graduates is not exhaustive, but it does suggest that graduates from HBCUs are making tremendous strides.

Par Excellence and Recommendation

Echoing Florida A&M University's motto, "Par Excellence with Caring," I would to recommend future scholars to carefully choose a post-secondary institution that offers a variety of majors and supports student needs. Students should also consider establishing a rapport with professors, administrators, and the local community. Additionally, developing your writing will open up opportunities to publish. Consider publishing at least two literary writings before graduating from graduate school, and present those papers at symposiums and conferences. Seek out internship and fellowship opportunities at corporations, foundations, government agencies, and nonprofit organizations. Maintain your focus, stay resilient, plan, prepare, produce, and reap that harvest of the plentiful seeds that will spring from your hard work. Furthermore, treat each person fairly regardless of his or her socio-economic background.

Perhaps the critics of HBCUs should consider that in life, "There is a time in every man's education when he arrives at the conviction that envy is ignorance; that imitation is suicide; that he must take himself for better, for worse, as his portion; that although the wide universe is full of good, no kernel of nourishing corn can come to him, but through his toil bestowed on that plot of ground, which is given to him to toll" (Emerson, 1841, para. 2). HBCU administrators, faculty, and students don't have to compete with Harvard, Yale, or Princeton. They provide a quality education to thousands of low- and moderate-income students from diverse backgrounds.

Conclusion

I truly believe that HBCUs, including Florida Agricultural and Mechanical and Clark Atlanta Universities, provide students with a foundation that cannot be replicated at PWIs. The faculty at Historically Black Colleges and Universities support students unconditionally, provide supportive environments, and educate students with various learning styles.

References

Baldwin, J. A. (1981). Notes on an Africentric theory of Black personality. *The Western Journal of Black Studies, 5*(3), 172–179.

Emerson, R. W. (1841). Self-reliance. Retrieved from http://www.emersoncentral.com/.com/Selfreliance.htm.com

Hine, D. C., Hine, W., & Harrold, S. (2010). *African-Americans: A concise history.* New Jersey: Pearson-Prentice Hall.

Jencks, C., & Riesman, D. (1968). *The academic revolution.* Chicago: University of Chicago Press.

Willie, C. (1979). Black colleges redefined. *Change* (October), 46–53.

Winthrop, J. (1977). *White over Black: American attitudes toward the Negro, 1550–1812.* New York: Norton.

11 A Liberating Spirituality
Evaluating Theological Education at a Black Graduate School

Herbert Robinson Marbury

The Interdenominational Theological Center, known as ITC by those in theological education, is known in other circles as "that radical preacher's school down in Atlanta." In the early 1990s I enrolled in ITC's master of divinity program, which is the foundational professional degree for ministry and broader religious leadership. I was drawn to the school both by its long and venerable history that began in Reconstruction and by my own family heritage. The origins of ITC's parent institutions (Gammon Theological Seminary—the United Methodist constituent founded in 1893; Morehouse School of Religion—the Baptist constituent founded in 1867; Turner Theological Seminary—the African Methodist Episcopal constituent founded in 1894; and Phillips School of Theology—the Christian Methodist Episcopal constituent founded in 1944) stretch back to the nineteenth century, but the school was formally constituted in 1958 during the upswing of the civil rights movement (*Interdenominational Theological Center: 1996 Alumni Directory*, 1997). In fact, one could argue that the same spirit of freedom that had inspired Black populations to coalesce into a national resistance movement brought these disparate schools together in Atlanta, which had long been a mecca for Black higher education.

Since Reconstruction, there had been many African American schools whose primary identity was shaped by their founding religious denominations. But in the late 1950s, the social and political landscape of the South rapidly changed for Black Americans. New challenges confronted Black communities and their churches. Only four years earlier, the Supreme Court's decision in *Brown vs. Board of Education of Topeka* traumatized White school districts across the nation, and Black communities experienced the backlash. Despite the new law of the land, White schools were unwilling to accept Black enrollees. Their administrators, teachers, and parents fought to preserve every inch of the segregation they had long enjoyed. Worse, the *Brown* decision led to the dissolution of many Black schools, which were cultural havens for Black students and struggling families. As Black schools disappeared, Black churches were left as one of the few remaining institutions where Black life could simply *be*—that is, free from a surveilling White gaze. However, the changing political and social landscape placed greater demand on Black churches and its leadership. Increasingly, congregations desired more than the type of pastoral leadership that focused their members on piety and discouraged communities from confronting injustice in the public sphere (Lincoln & Mamiya, 1990). Martin Luther King Jr., Fannie Lou Hamer, Ralph Abernathy, Andrew Young, and other activists appeared as the new models for clergy and religious leadership (Baldwin, 1991). No longer was it adequate to educate Black clergy whose primary allegiance and religious formation was located in their Methodist, Baptist, or other denominational traditions. So, when the four constituent seminaries came together to form a new institution for theological education in the South, Black solidarity in service of the Black church rather than denominational identity stood at the center of its ecumenical origins.

Black churches had become the organizing center of the new victories of the civil rights movement. ITC envisioned itself as providing rigorous and relevant theological education that would enable Black churches and their communities to seize this new horizon. ITC would serve the age by preparing clergy to lead Black communities and their churches.

As important as ITC's history was in influencing my decision to enroll, so was my own family heritage. Long before the constituent schools came together, Gammon Theological Seminary, one of ITC's parent institutions, had trained Black clergy for almost a century (McClain, 1984). These included several members of my family. My father, grandfather, and several uncles were all "Gammon Men"—educated in Historically Black Colleges and Universities (HBCUs) and trained to lead the Black church. My education, however, was different. I matriculated at Emory University, a predominantly White United Methodist school with its own graduate school of theology. During my senior year as an undergraduate, I announced to my family that I had accepted my call to ministry. The moment both affirmed their long-held hope that God would call a minister in the family's next generation, but it also sparked a deep fear that I would continue to pursue my education at a majority White institution. It was then that my great uncle immediately interjected, "It's about time you left that 'buckra school' and come on home to Gammon-ITC." I agreed.

For four years Emory had given me a very good education, and the Black community there, at the time, was close-knit and supportive. Nonetheless, something was missing. So as a graduating senior I wholeheartedly agreed with my uncle, although I never articulated it. Now, years later, time and distance have clarified and perhaps tempered some of my angst. In the HBCU students who visited our campus, I believed that I recognized a clue to what I missed. Emory was located just minutes from the Atlanta University Center, so students from Clark Atlanta University, Spelman College, Morris Brown College, and Morehouse College were always visiting our campus and vice versa. Whereas their schools may not have provided the kind of material resources that Emory afforded us, they possessed a particular self-confidence and cultural grounding that I envied. At the time, I attributed their affect to what I believed was "the HBCU" undergraduate experience. I imagined that it was the fruit of four years of study free of demonstrating to White students, faculty, and administrators the worthiness of one's place of admission. It meant the ability to be fully and simply a student without ever taking on the subject position of "representing your race" in response to incessant inquiries about anything Black. My sentiment echoed Toni Morrison's well-known pronouncement that "the function, the very serious function of racism is distraction. It keeps you from doing your work. It keeps you explaining, over and over again, your reason for being."[1]

Such was the hope that I carried with me when I arrived at ITC as a first-year student. By then, the '60s had long passed. The urgent spirit of that age, which had given birth to the civil rights and Black power movements, and to ITC as well, had now abated. But racialization in its myriad pernicious forms still plagued Black life. The times had changed, but the need for the type of theological relevance in training Black religious leadership that ITC fulfilled remained. Indeed, some of the important victories of 1960s had already begun to be rolled by back under the Nixon administration and then later the Reagan-Bush administrations. Many of the expectations that the movements of the 1960s raised had been dashed. The ensuing years had not finished bringing about the sweeping qualitative change in the lives of Black communities that the reforms of the 1960s had promised. In fact, Black life languished under the resurgence of the conservatism of the 1980s. Black churches had not fared much better. By the 1980s less than 20 percent of Black clergy had completed the kind of professional degree in theological education that intended to prepare them to lead local churches (Lincoln & Mamiya, 1990). So for ITC, the mission that began in 1958 did not end with the era of civil rights gains; it only adapted to the changing landscape of racialization.

From the moment I sat in my first course, a sense of the familiar washed over me and I exhaled. As I looked up and down the rows of the class, I saw a plurality of Black life represented; I no longer had to be the only one as I had been in many of my undergraduate courses. More significantly, in that class I saw clearly ITC's vision of leading the Black church. It meant stretching the church's imagination beyond the traditional embodiment of leaders who were male, married, and heterosexual. Whereas such has generally been the representation of the Black church's leadership, the makeup of the membership was always different. More often, the majority of Black church rolls comprised women rather than men, who were single rather than married. Moreover, members of Black LGBT communities often served in various ministries, although their identities were generally unarticulated. The composition of the ITC student body included people from all walks of life. Indeed, ITC's commitment to educate leaders extended to the entire Black church, and its many communities, not simply to those whom the church had historically privileged.

A school's commitments are reflected not only in the character of its student body but in its curriculum; this was particularly true for ITC. Typically, majority White schools of theological education structure curricula and pedagogies to educate the average student of a generation ago—White, male, newly or soon-to-be married (so that his wife cared for his children while he matriculated full-time). Students trained to lead a "large-steeple" middle-class churches in suburbia. The gospel they prepared to preach offered little challenge to the social, political, and economic realities that structured a world of white privilege. Questions such as, "What does God have to say about disparities in access to health care, education and the ongoing menace of police brutality?" rarely, if at all, entered the conversation. However, at ITC, the pedagogy and curriculum engaged these matters head-on. In other words, in each class, the gospel of Jesus Christ had everything to say about the realities of Black life.

My first course, biblical studies, illustrated this difference. A course in biblical studies is traditionally foundational for any curriculum in theological education. But as one can imagine, the content of such a course varies depending on the theological orientation, denominational affiliation, and social, cultural, and political commitments of the professor or institution, among others. Moreover, the Bible and its meanings are culturally and historically contingent; in other words, meanings absolutely depend on the communities that are reading the scriptures. This was as true both for White Christians in the antebellum South who emphasized scriptures such as "slaves, obey your earthly masters with fear and trembling . . ." (Ephesians 6:5), which affirmed slavery, and for abolitionists who read scriptures such as, "For freedom Christ has set us free. Stand firm, therefore, and do not submit again to a yoke of slavery" (Galatians 5:1), and fight vehemently against the slave regime (Marbury, 2015). At ITC, biblical studies courses focused on reading the Bible in ways that were both relevant to affirming the beauty and the power that God had created in Black life and in ways that were useful for confronting the ongoing challenges that Black life faced.

Dr. Randall C. Bailey, the senior Old Testament professor, taught my biblical studies course. In addition to being a scholar, he was a Baptist minister with deep roots in Black church and had a history of fighting for civil and human rights. His political and theological orientation were in line with both the institution's and my own. It was the first time in my life that I had experienced such a level of resonance. In other words, we could engage in the process of learning without the added burden of changing or translating cultural codes or personal histories or hedging on our theological and political commitments.

In that semester we spent a fair amount of time on the book of Exodus. For Americans, Exodus is probably one of the most formational stories for the new republic (Byrd, 2013). Using figural readings, Puritans read Exodus and saw themselves as the Israelites escaping bondage in Europe and establishing a promised land in the New World. Through the biblical story, they took up Native American peoples as "Canaanites" whose cultures were abominations in the New World (Coffey, 2013). Such readings of the Bible, along with the impulses of colonialism, led to the genocidal practices enacted upon Native American peoples in North America.

Exodus figures prominently in African American cultural life as well. However, Americans' interpretation and historical performance focused on Exodus 1 through 14, the escape from Egypt rather than the conquest of a Promised Land.[2] The Bible has been central to Black religious expression since the first enslaved Africans arrived. Not long after hearing the Bible's stories and later reading them, Black people were drawn to the book of Exodus and to Moses as liberator. Exodus became the paradigmatic story of freedom from bondage. Its symbols became the language for articulating meaning for Black people's experience, from Harriet Tubman, who was commonly called "the Moses of her people," to Martin Luther King Jr., who, on the night before his assassination, took on the persona of Moses, exclaiming, "I've looked over and I've seen the Promised Land" (Callahan, 2006; Wimbush, 1991).

Many of us were familiar with this cultural history of Exodus, and most saw the Children of Israel's enslavement in Egypt and freedom beyond the Red Sea as an analogue to the perpetual subjugation and struggles for freedom that characterized African American history. However, for Dr. Bailey, such a reading alone removes one's focus from the reality of Black life in the United States. Pointing the class to the parallels between the story's portrayal of the Canaanites and our own history, he called the class to re-read the story from the Canaanites' perspective (Bailey, 1995, 1998). They were a free people who lived peacefully on ancestral land for generations. In the story, the Israelites invaded Canaan, bringing with them the violent practices of war such as enslavement and rape. They justified the conquest by claiming that they acted at God's direction. As a first-year seminarian, the parallels were chilling. What was more distressing was that in years of reading the Bible, I had not seen them myself. As the course continued, we learned that Bailey's reading was, in fact, in line with the readings of Native Americans and Black South Africans (Mosala, 1989; Warrior, 2006).

Whereas Bailey's class expanded our worldview to see ourselves as a part of a global community and to see our interests in common with other marginalized people, ITC's curriculum encouraged real-life cross-cultural engagement. ITC's vision of the Black church extended to the African Diaspora, and so there were many opportunities to make cultural and religious connections with communities on the continent and throughout other parts of the Black Atlantic.[3] We were encouraged to see our struggles and the interests of our communities in common with Black communities in places such as the Caribbean, Africa, and South America. During my second year in the program, I participated in a summer immersion course led by Dr. Ndugu G. B. T'Ofori-Atta, who directed Religious Heritage and the African World Center, one of the cocurricular programs at ITC. (The fact that such a program existed in an institution of theological education spoke to deep commitments characterized by its HBCU identity.) It was my first time in the Motherland. We traveled to Ghana and engaged communities in Accra, Cape Coast, and Kumasi. Unlike White missionaries of an earlier generation, we did not go to teach or to convert. We went to reconnect as family members whom history had rendered asunder. So our perspective was different than that of some others from majority institutions. In Ghana, we encountered the God of our ancestors in African Traditional Religions. We mapped the legacies of those beliefs and practices, which are still present in many Black American worship experiences. We also encountered the legacy of colonialism Ghana reflected in the face of every "white Jesus" that appeared in shops, restaurants, and what seemed like the back of each taxi. We realized our shared legacy of colonialism.

Throughout the course, we spent much of our time engaged in cross-cultural dialogs with Christian communities. Our professors led us in discussions that gave us context for our subject positionality as one among many communities of practitioners of Christianity in the African Diaspora with a common religious heritage and common interests. Although much of West African Christianity springs from the work of Western missionaries, the differences in practices and fundamental beliefs was startling. I began to realize that religions take on the character of the societies of the people who practice them. So much of what I had grown up believing was orthodox Christian practice was actually the ways that the religion had been adapted for our Western context. I learned that religious practice and belief is always culturally specific. For example, North American Christianity is different in practice and in theology from practices and beliefs among Christian communities in South America, in Africa, and in Asia. Even in the United States, the cultural differences between African American, Latino, and White communities shape fundamental differences in practice and theology. No religion is a "one-size fits all" template. So it became important for us take seriously our cultures and the religious needs of the communities that formed us and to take seriously the needs and cultures of those communities whom we were called to serve. I left Ghana with a broader and critically richer perspective on my faith.

Both my descriptions of the coursework and the cocurricular program are indicative of the educational experience that ITC afforded me. That education has been invaluable for the work to which I have been called in ministry, first as a pastor and chaplain, and second as a professor who educates students preparing for ministry.

Since graduating from ITC, my call to ministry has taken three forms. In each, my ITC education has proven invaluable. During my final year in the master's program, I was appointed to serve as pastor of Old National United Methodist Church in Riverdale, Georgia. The congregation had struggled due to bureaucratic issues both at the conference and local church levels. At the time of my appointment, my bishop expected the church to close at the next annual conference. Nonetheless, they needed a pastor until then, and he thought I would gain some very good experience during the year. With only a year to work before the church was slated to disband, I immediately contacted other ITC alumni who had begun their ministries in similar circumstances. I recalled my deep immersion in classes that studied the character the Black community life, so I turned to the barber and beauty shops and other local establishments to raise visibility for the church in that community. Although I was not conscious of it at the time, the ITC name granted me a measure of goodwill as I worked. Members of the community recognized its alumni as ministers of high caliber and high character. During the rest of my time at Old National United Methodist Church, I strived to live up to both. With a some mentoring from other ITC alumni, reliance on my Black church administration course, and most importantly a congregation that was willing to work hard toward its own growth, the church quadrupled in attendance in five years, constructed an edifice, and became a vital part of its community.

Soon after the congregation was well established, I left to begin doctoral studies in religion at Vanderbilt University. I had been strongly influenced by the work of Randall C. Bailey, my seminary professor, and I had a deep desire to become a scholar and to participate in educating those preparing for ministry. By the end of my first year at ITC, I had indicated to my professors that I intended to pursue a PhD. Instead of evaluating my worthiness for such an endeavor, they responded by mentoring me and developing my potential. My professors provided me with essential reading lists and individualized courses whose rigor simulated that of the most elite doctoral programs, from which many of them had graduated. ITC had a long history of preparing students for doctoral work. In fact, Bailey had already prepared several students for doctoral studies and had sent two to Vanderbilt before me. Again, ITC's reputation preceded me. Once I arrived at Vanderbilt, I was introduced to a community of Black doctoral students who were studying at fine schools located around the country, including a few at Vanderbilt. Our areas of academic pursuit and interest were vastly different, but we had one common bond—we were prepared by ITC.

My relationship with ITC provided me with professional opportunities beyond parish ministry. After leaving residency in the doctoral program, Dr. L. Henry Whelchel invited me to apply for the university chaplain's position at Clark Atlanta University. Dr. Whelchel had been one of my professors at ITC but had moved on to become chair of the Religion and Philosophy Department at Clark Atlanta. He and the Reverend Paul Easley, the former chaplain and another graduate of ITC, had heard about my work at Old National United Methodist Church and wanted to see a revitalization of the religious life program at CAU.

At the time CAU was the largest of the private HBCUs. The position was a huge step for me. I was appointed to rebuild the religious life program, to set a vision, a mission, and to develop the personnel and programmatic resources to fulfill them. I inherited a program that garnered participation from fifteen to twenty students on a weekly basis. Within two years we increased our staff by sixfold by collaborating with the Interdenominational Theological Center and Candler School of Theology at Emory University. By the end of the second year, our weekly programming garnered the participation of more than five hundred members of the community weekly, which was three times the national average for a campus of forty-five hundred students. Much of the success was due to my formation at ITC. The students who participated in religious life at CAU had grown up in the same communities represented by the Black churches that ITC had trained me to serve. They, similar to the student body at ITC, represented a plurality of Black life.

When I left Clark Atlanta to join the faculty at Vanderbilt, I was sure that I would draw upon my doctoral education more than anything else for my work as a scholar. In part, that is true in all of the obvious ways—research, theory, methods, and so forth. However, I had not anticipated how much pedagogy required of me to integrate subject content with real, lived experience. Mastering the canons of our disciplines was but a baseline expectation. The students I encounter wanted *paideia*—that is an experience that shapes values and character as *Wissenschaft*, intellectual content. They were interested in how my experience had informed what I taught and vice versa. In fact, this is one of the goals of theological education.

For the remainder of the twenty-first century the shifting sociocultural milieu makes the kind of theological education ITC offers more valuable than ever. Religious practice and belief arise from a deep embeddedness within a culture. The increase in Black and Latino populations in the United States over the next few decades will demand scholars, clergy, and other religious leadership who are educated to ask the critical questions, produce the literature, and lead the religious communities that fulfill their cultural expectations. Those preparing to be relevant in the next decades should bring the kinds of education and cultural formation that will reflect the global landscape to come.

Notes

1. The quote is from a speech by Toni Morrison entitled, "A Humanist View." It was delivered as a part of the "Black Studies Center public dialogue. Pt. 2," on May 30, 1975 at Portland State University.
2. The focus on the escape from Egypt rather than the conquest is partly due to Black people's perpetual oppression by ever-adapting forms of racialization in the US (the slave regime, Black Codes, and Jim Crow, among others). Also, Black people in the US had nowhere to go, no Promised Land to which an exodus might lead. Instead, formerly enslaved Africans had little choice but to remain and build a life among their former oppressors. For examples of interpretive activity on Exodus, see the work of Absalom Jones and David Walker in the Colonial period (Hinks, 2008; Jones, 1995); Frances Ellen Watkins Harper and John Jasper during Reconstruction (Harper, 1869; Jasper, 1908); Zora Neale Hurston and James Weldon Johnson in the Harlem Renaissance (Johnson, 2000); and Albert Cleage in the era of the Black Power Movement (Cleage, 1989).

3. The term "Black Atlantic" refers to Paul Gilroy's concept of common cultural formations of people of African descent produced by modernity and shared black peoples in the Americas, Britain, and the Caribbean.(Gilroy, 1993).

References

Bailey, R. C. (1995). They're nothing but incestuous bastards: The polemical use of sex and sexuality in Hebrew canon narratives. In F. F. Segovia & M. A. Tolbert (Eds.), *Reading from this place: Social location and Biblical interpretation in the United States* (pp. 121–138). (Vol. 1). Minneapolis: Fortress Press.

Bailey, R. C. (1998). The danger of ignoring one's own cultural bias. In R. S. Sugirtharajah (Ed.), *The Postcolonial Bible* (pp. 66–90). Sheffield: Sheffield Academic Press.

Baldwin, L. V. (1991). *There is a balm in Gilead: The cultural roots of Martin Luther King, Jr*. Minneapolis: Fortress Press.

Byrd, J. P. (2013). *Sacred scripture, sacred war: The Bible and the American revolution*. New York: Oxford.

Callahan, A. D. (2006). *The talking book: African Americans and the Bible*. New Haven: Yale University Press.

Cleage, A. B. (1989). *The Black Messiah*. Trenton, NJ: Africa World Press.

Coffey, J. (2013). *Exodus and liberation: Deliverance politics from John Calvin to Martin Luther King Jr*. New York: Oxford.

Gilroy, P. (1993). *The Black Atlantic: Modernity and double consciousness*. Cambridge, MA: Harvard University Press.

Harper, F. E. W. (1869). *Moses: Story of the Nile*. Philadelphia: Merrihew and Son.

Hinks, P. P. (Ed.). (2008). *David Walker's appeal to the coloured citizens of the world*. Univeristy Park, PA: Pennsylvania State University Press.

Interdenominational Theological Center: 1996 alumni directory. (1997). Holiday, FL: Alumni Research, Inc.

Jasper, J. (1908). The sun do move. In W. E. Hatcher (Ed.), *John Jasper: The unmatched Negro philosopher and preacher* (pp. 133–149). New York: Fleming H. Revell Company.

Johnson, J. W. (2000). *James Weldon Johnson: Complete poems*. New York: Penguin.

Jones, A. (1995). A thanksgiving sermon. In D. Porter (Ed.), *Early Negro writing 1760–1837* (pp. 335–342). Philadelphia: Black Classic Press.

Lincoln, C. E., & Mamiya, L. H. (1990). *The Black church in the African American experience*. Durham, NC: Duke University Press.

Marbury, H. R. (2015). *Pillars of cloud and fire: The politics of exodus in African American Biblical interpretaion*. New York: New York University Press.

McClain, W. B. (1984). *Black people in the Methodist church: Whither thou goest?* Cambridge, MA: Schenkman Publishing Company.

Mosala, I. (1989). *Biblical hermeneutics and Black theology in South Africa*. Grand Rapids, MI: Eerdmans.

Warrior, R. A. (2006). Canaanites, cowboys, and Indians. In R. S. Sugirtharajah (Ed.), *Voices from the margin interpreting the Bible in the Third World* (pp. 235–241). Maryknoll, NY: Orbis Books.

Wimbush, V. (1991). The Bible and African Americans: An outline of an interpretive history. In C. H. Felder (Ed.), *Stony the road we trod: African American Biblical interpretation* (pp. 81–97). Minneapolis: Fortress Press.

12 Strange Fruit

The Contribution of the Historically Black College and University (HBCU) to the Development of the Black Intelligentsia

F. Abron Franklin

Prior to and since the days of slavery, the African American has been seen as the "other" or as an inapposite being within civil society, whose subhuman existence warranted little to no regard. The lived experience of the African American reflects a social structural trajectory designed to subjugate him to a status of invisibility. The civil rights movement addresses the contours of this violative architecture by acting as an apparatus to thwart the assaultive animus of slavery, the Black codes of the nineteenth century, Jim Crow segregation, and the lack of equal opportunity under the law. The opportunity to access equitable education remained an entrenched and protracted issue for the civil rights movement until the United States Supreme Court unanimously held that the "separate but equal" doctrine was impermissible under the Constitution's Fourteenth Amendment.

In the tradition of the subaltern lens, the Black intellectual is also seen as an inapposite phenomenon or a paradoxical conundrum (Spivak, 1988; West, 1985). African Americans have been and arguably, in some cases, still are considered intellectually inferior to their White counterparts (Posnock, 1997). In spite of the traditional value of education within the African American community or the collective efforts of African Americans to ensure equal access to education, the myth of intellectual inferiority persists (Cokley, 2003). Accordingly, African Americans inherently lack the capacity to substantively contribute to the intellectual enterprise. In response to this contemptuous philosophical worldview, Historically Black Colleges and Universities (HBCU) were established to address the systematic and systemic social discrimination against African Americans in pursuit of higher education.

Historically Black Colleges and Universities provide the requisite communal space to engage the intellectual development of the African American student (Du Bois, 1903). Although credence has been given to the utility and necessity of this space regarding the academic development of the undergraduate student, less attention has been given to place and space of the HBCU in the development of the African American graduate or professional student. The purpose of this essay is to initiate a reflective articulation of my motivation to attend an HBCU for postgraduate education and highlight the contributory role of the Historically Black College and University in the development of a Black intelligentsia.

The Uneducated Slave

Before the Civil War, slavery and segregation prevented the African American from accessing educational opportunities. The end of the American Civil War marked a new chapter in the life of the African American. The Thirteenth, Fourteenth, and Fifteenth Amendments emancipated African Americans and established high right of citizenship. The emancipation of the African American from slavery resulted in 4.4 million free African Americans (Williams & Ashley, 2004). Among this new citizenry, given of the conspiratorial practices of Whites to keep African Americans ignorant by legally forbidding the education of slaves, 92 percent had spent their entire lives as slaves, and the literacy rate was 5 percent (Drewry & Doermann, 2001). In response, the US Bureau of Refugees, Freedmen, and Abandoned Lands, otherwise known as the Freedmen's Bureau, was established in 1865 by Congress to assist former African American slaves and poor Whites in the South. A primary role of the bureau was to help former slaves in their aspiration to find homes, obtain employment, and establish schools.

African Americans seized every opportunity to invest in education by advancing from the clandestine educational practices that functioned during slavery to developing formal structures to support the education of the Negro. The post–Civil War establishment of elementary and secondary education was painstakingly slow in the South. Southern landowners and the South's broader body politic objected to the idea of free public schools for any racial group. Notwithstanding the desire to learn, the aspiration of the African American to be formally educated was also met with civil discord. A 1968 report of the Freedman's Bureau established numerous crimes against individuals attempting to educate African Americans (Williams & Ashley, 2004). In one case, in Williamson County, Texas, a school, under the direction of an African American woman named Laura Eggleston, was decimated by fire in the middle of the night, and in Falls County, Texas, a teacher was murdered by a local group in opposition to the education of African Americans.

The judiciary also played an instrumental role in ensuring the Negro would remain uneducated. State laws classified African Americans as personal property or as chattel and made it illegal to teach the slave to read or write. The case of *Dred Scott v. Sanford* furthered the denial of citizenship to African Americans. Decided in 1857, the landmark case involved Scott, a slave, who claimed a right to his freedom because his master had taken him from Missouri, a slave state, to the free states of Illinois and Wisconsin. The court denied Scott's claim that he had become free when he was taken into and/or lived in a free territory. The significance of the Scott holding was that, regardless of being enslaved or free, an African American could not be a citizen, and consequently, he had no standing to make a claim in federal court. Moreover, the federal government lacked the authority to regulate slavery in any territories acquired after the establishment of the United States.

Plessy v. Ferguson was the next legal case to further eradicate the African American citizenship status. In 1892, Homer Plessy, while on board a railroad car in the state of Louisiana, which had passed legislation mandating the railroads provide separate cars for Blacks and Whites, was asked to move from a railroad car designated for Whites, and Plessy refused to do so. Plessy's refusal resulted in his arrest, and in response; Plessy claimed the violation of his Thirteenth Amendment rights and his equal protection guarantee under the Fourteenth Amendment. In 1896, the US Supreme Court heard the Plessy challenge, and the Court upheld the constitutionality of the state law mandating racial segregation in public facilities under the infamous legal doctrine of "separate but equal." Although initially the *Plessy* ruling was intended for public facilities, racial animus promoted an interpretive scope inclusive of public education. In totality, the holdings of *Dredd Scott* and *Plessy* legally relegated the African American to a status of the "other" wholly marginalized and therefore, warranting no place, equal or otherwise, in the democratic republic.

African Americans and Higher Education

At the turn of the twentieth century, African Americans developed significant strides toward securing access to higher education. The first college for African Americans, now known as Cheyney State University, was in established in 1837, in Pennsylvania; however, twenty-five years after the Civil War, there were approximately one hundred colleges and universities for African Americans, which were predominantly in the South (Allen & Jewell, 2002; Brown & Davis, 2001). By 1890, over two hundred HBCUs were established by philanthropic organizations, churches, missionaries, private donors, and local communities. Through the middle of the twentieth century, over 90 percent of African American students enrolled in higher education in the US were educated at Historically Black Colleges and Universities (HBCUs) (Kim & Conrad, 2006). Despite the decline in enrollment in HBCUs since the 1960s, among African American college graduates, a disproportionately greater number of political leaders, lawyers, doctors, and PhD recipients are HBCU graduates. Although the one hundred or so current HBCUs represent approximately 3 percent of the American colleges and universities, they enroll an estimated 20 percent of all African American college students (Allen, Jewell, Griffin, & Wolf, 2007). Simply put, HBCUs are the primary producers of African American scholars to go forward to become leaders in their communities. An estimated 15 percent of master's degrees, 10 percent of doctorates, and 15 percent of first professional degrees are conferred upon African American students from HBCUs. Accordingly, as late as the

1990s, 52 percent of African American pharmacy degree recipients, 30 percent of dentistry degree recipients, and 27 percent of theology degree recipients were educated at an HBCU (Redd, 1998).

The 1954 Supreme Court decision in *Brown v. Board of Education* was pivotal in American history because it fundamentally transformed the nation's relationship to the education of its citizenry by directly challenging the inequalities in education propagated by the legal doctrines of *Scott* and *Plessy*. The *Brown* ruling mandated the racial integration of public elementary and secondary schools. *Brown* provided the legal framework and a counternarrative to the proposition of "separate but equal" as a constructive truth. Moreover, *Brown* put forth a foundation for subsequent court rulings to eliminate the racial segregation of public colleges and universities in the South. Prior to the Brown decision, 90 percent of the African American college and university enrollment was attributed to HBCUs (Allen et al., 2007; Drewry & Doermann, 2001). After the *Brown* decision, a larger number of institutions of higher education were available to African American students. By 1970, the proportion of African American college and university enrollment at the HBCU diminished to 48 percent. The enrollment in HBCUs would not rise again to record levels until the 1990s (Drewry & Doermann, 2001).

Black College Aspirations

I was a part of the 1990s enrollment resurgence of Historically Black Colleges and Universities (HBCUs). In 1988, I entered Morgan State University as a freshman science major. It was the HBCU undergraduate experience that informed my decision to engage my initial postgraduate training at an HBCU; hence, I obtained a master of public health (MPH) degree from the Morehouse School of Medicine. My decision to attend an HBCU for my undergraduate education was thoughtfully intentional. As a high school senior, I applied to approximately ten colleges, all of which were HBCU institutions.

The vestiges of my middle school and high school experiences can be tied back to the legacy of school busing. Although I enjoyed my tenure in both middle and high school, I left that experience with a burning desire to ensure that my college experience would be nothing short of Black. The choice to attend an HBCU was tied to the connection between the HBCU and the civil rights movement of the 1950s and the 1960s. Moreover, I came to a burgeoning realization of the potential role of HBCUs in the post-civil rights era.

Historically Black Colleges and Universities (HBCUs) were at the center of the civil rights movement (Allen & Jewell, 2002; Kilson, 2014). During the movement, HBCUs made significant contributions to the deconstruction of racial barriers to education and to the overall advancement of civil rights. HBCUs provided the instrumental leadership and the requisite front-line staff necessary to sustain the movement. HBCU alumni were represented in the leadership of civil rights organizations and stood out among the many attorneys who strategized and litigated on behalf of the disenfranchised. As an institution, in many instances, the HBCU provided the credentialed intelligentsia equipped to leverage the social capital derived from hard-fought advances (Allen et al., 2007). HBCU graduates were more likely to be represented among the African Americans trailblazers in occupational fields that were traditionally closed to African Americans.

The HBCU context became an incubator for political activism and social justice (Williams & Ashley, 2004). For example, Julian Bond established the Committee on Appeal for Human Rights (COAHR) while attending Morehouse College in 1960. As a student at Howard University, Stokely Carmichael, who later became Kwame Toure', participated in organized student protests against segregated facilities.

Marion Write Edelman, while a student at Spelman College, was motivated to become a civil rights attorney due the dearth of lawyers available to represent poor African Americans. Additional activists who attended HBCUs include Medgar Evers (Alcorn State University); Martin Luther King Jr. (Morehouse College); Langston Hughes and Thurgood Marshal (Lincoln University of Pennsylvania); Zora Neale Hurston and E. Franklin Frazier (Howard University); and the list goes on.

Regarding the nexus between civil rights and the HBCU, Charles Hamilton Houston made an indelible impression and cemented my desire to attend an HBCU. Charles Hamilton Houston was a scholar, educator, and lawyer, and he fiercely committed his life to extinguishing racism and the social structures that supported and reinforced racial animus by using the rule of law as instrument for justice and social change (Biography.com). I initially discovered Houston's work in my reading of the book *Eyes on the Prize*, by Juan Williams, and through subsequent research. Charles Hamilton Houston was a 1915 graduate of Amherst College and a 1922 graduate of Harvard Law School. Again, in 1923, Houston graduated from Harvard Law earning the Doctor of Juridicial Science (SJD). Although Houston was not a graduate of an HBCU, his life's work and advocacy for social justice is imbued in the bricks, mortar, and spirit of Howard University School of Law (HUSL). Houston is credited for developing the Howard University Legal Department into a fully accredited law school, which is the oldest of the Historically Black Law Schools (HBLS). Houston is also credited with establishing the Legal Defense Fund of the National Association of the Advancement of Color People (NAACP).

Charles Hamilton Houston's most storied contribution to the law and the civil rights movement was the dismantling of the "separate but equal" legal doctrine (McNeil, 2011). The doctrine served as the architectural reasoning of the "Jim Crow" laws that dictated racial segregation in public facilities and in education (i.e., primary, secondary, and higher education). Earlier civil rights case law, established by Houston, was critically necessary for developing the legal strategy behind *Brown v. Board of Education*. The two cases, *Murray v. Pearson* and *Missouri ex rel. Gaines v. Canada*, initiated the erosion of the "separate but equal" standard. Each case involved an African American plaintiff challenging a denied entry into a racially segregated law school (i.e., University of Maryland and University of Missouri, respectively). Following are the words of Charles Hamilton Houston, which guide the mission of HUSL:

> *[the] Negro lawyer must be trained as a social engineer and group interpreter. Due to the Negro's social and political condition . . . the Negro must be prepared to anticipate, guide and interpret his group advancement . . . [Moreover, he must act as] business advisor . . . for the protection of the scattered resources possessed or controlled by the group . . . He must provide more ways and means for holding within the group the income now flowing through it. A lawyer is either a social engineer or he's a parasite on society[. . .]*

Understanding Houston's work, his mentorship of Thurgood Marshall, and the interconnectedness between these two individuals and the HBCU, it became undeniably clear that I had to be a part of the HBCU experience, and I wanted the HBCU experience to be a part of me.

The HBCU Graduate Education

The experiential benefits of an undergraduate education informed my decision to pursue graduate-level training of a professional master's degree. Compared to predominantly White universities (PWIs), HBCUs are better at promoting the development and growth of the African American student (Berger & Milem, 2000). Specifically, more often, the HBCU environment is conducive to promoting the concept of self. Self-concept takes into consideration the following: (1) psychosocial wellness; (2) achievement orientation; and (3) academic ability. The psychosocial wellness dimension includes emotional and physical health, social and intellectual self-confidence, understanding of others, and cooperativeness. Attending an HBCU was the strongest predictor of psychosocial wellness for African American students compared to African American students at a PWI. Although the HBCU institution often has fewer material resources compared to their predominately White counterparts, the HBCU successfully graduates an equivalent number of, if not more, African American students (Kim & Conrad, 2006). The HBCU provides a more collegial and supportive learning environment.

As it relates to HBCUs and their historic focus on the education of African American students, HBCUs have six unique goals: (1) the maintenance of the African American historical and cultural influences emanating from the African American community; (2) the provision of key leadership for the African American community given the important social role of university administrators, scholars, and students engaged in community affairs (e.g., a paragon of social organization); (3) the provision of economic function within the African American community; (4) the provision of African American role models to interpret the way in which social, political, and economic dynamics impact African American people; (5) the provision of college graduates with a distinct competence to address the issues between the minority and nonminority population groups; and (6) the production of African American agents for specialized research, institutional training, and information dissemination in dealing with the lived experience of African American and other minority communities. Embedded in the goals endemic to the HBCU is the idea of leadership and generators of knowledge.

The graduate experience at an HBCU either further engenders or perhaps inculcates an ethno-ideological centered form of leadership and advances a safe space to promote the intellectual imagination and intellectual resiliency of the African American graduate student (Du Bois, 1903; Kilson, 2014). The leadership function impressed upon the African American graduate student can be characterized by what anthropologists or sociologists call "social organization." Social organization implies the ability of a community or collective structure to realize the common values of its members and leverage levels of social control or agency to acquire productive means of social capital.

Social organization implicates the principles of social-organizational leadership, which, at the HBCU, is concerned with building up the institutional infrastructure of an ethnic group development by nurturing or cultivating agencies such as churches, trade, unions, civic aid societies, and fraternal/sororal associations (Kilson, 2014).

The social-organizational leadership was characterized by W.E.B. Du Bois as mobilization-type leadership (i.e., civil rights activism) (Kilson, 2014). For Du Bois, this type of leadership was indispensable to the principles of progressive African American leadership that exist for and within the larger African American context, regardless of class. Under an Emersonian ethos, the African American intellectual has the moral imperative and attribute of unmasking and challenging inequality. The HBCU graduate experience instills an African-American communitarian leadership, which promotes a duty among the trained African American scholar to use his intellectual capabilities to advance an interclass social mobilization commensurate with the overall interest of the collective. The African American communitarian leadership activism emphasizes that the HBCU graduate has a special obligation and responsibility to engage in outreach of the broader community to assist in its advancement.

There is a visceral connection between the faculty and the student at an HBCU institution. The connection stems from the fact that, at an HBCU, the faculty and staff intrinsically tie their success to the success of the students. Compared to material or quantitative resources, which can be disconnected from the human experience, this connection translates into a qualitatively distinct currency for the student.

The currency communicates a committed sense of trust, belief, and positive expectations of the student's ability to succeed and inherently, the connection between the faculty, staff, and the student in the HBCU community supports a global mentoring environment for the African American student. In addition to providing an anti-intellectual counternarrative (Cokley, 2003), the HBCU acts as a unique source of social capital among the African American community (Brown & Davis, 2001). Given the unequalled constellation of African American intellectuals and professionals produced by the HBCU (Kilson, 2014), the HBCU acts a conduit for the manufacturing and disseminating social capital to its African American students.

References

Allen, W. R., & Jewell, J. O. (2002). A backward glance forward: Past, present and future perspectives on historically Black colleges and universities. *The Review of Higher Education, 25*(3), 241–261.

Allen, W. R., Jewell, J. O., Griffin, K. A., & Wolf, D. S. (2007). Historically Black colleges and universities: Honoring the past, engaging the present, touching the future. *The Journal of Negro Education, 76*(3), 263–280.

Berger, J. B., & Milem, J. F. (2000). Exploring the impact of historically Black colleges in promoting the development of undergraduates' self-concept. *Journal of College Student Development, 41*(4), 1–14.

Brown, M. C., & Davis, J. E. (2001). The historically Black college as social contract, social capital, and social equalizer. *Peabody Journal of Education, 76*(1), 31–49.

Cokley, K. O. (2003). What do we know about the motivation of African American students? Challenging the "anti-intellectual" myth. *Harvard Educational Review, 73*(4), 524–558.

Drewry, H. N., & Doermann, H. (2001). *Stand and prosper: Private Black colleges and their students*. Princeton, NJ: Princeton University Press.

Du Bois, W. E. B. (1903). *The souls of Black folk*. Oxford University Press.

Kilson, M. (2014). *Transformation of the African American intelligentsia 1800–2012*. Cambridge, MA: Harvard University Press.

Kim, M. M., & Conrad, C. F. (2006). The impact of historically Black colleges and universities on the academic success of African-American students. *Research in Higher Education, 47*(4), 399–427.

McNeil, G. R. (2011). *Groundwork: Charles Hamilton Houston and the struggle for civil rights*. Philadelphia, PA: University of Pennsylvania Press.

Posnock, R. (1997). How it feels to be a problem: Du Bois, Fanon, and the "impossible life" of the Black intellectual. *Critical Inquiry, 23*(2), 323–349.

Redd, K. E. (1998). Historically Black colleges and universities: Making a comeback. *New Directions for Higher Education, 102*, 33–43.

Spivak, G. (1988). Can the subaltern speak? In C. Nelson & L. Grossberg (Eds.), *Marxism interpretations of culture* (pp. 271–313). Basingstoke: Macmillian Education.

West, C. (1985). The dilemma of the Black intellectual. *Cultural Critique, 1*, 109–124.

Williams, J., & Ashley, D. (2004). *I'll find a way or make one: A tribute to historically Black colleges and universities*. New York: Harper Collins.

About the Editors

Dr. Robert T. Palmer is an associate professor in the Department of Educational Leadership and Policy Studies at Howard University. His research examines issues of access, equity, retention, persistence, and the college experience of racial and ethnic minorities, particularly within the context of Historically Black Colleges and Universities. Dr. Palmer's work has been published in leading journals in higher education, such as *The Journal of College Student Development, Teachers College Record, Journal of Diversity in Higher Education, Journal of Negro Education, College Student Affairs Journal, Journal of College Student Retention, The Negro Educational Review*, and *Journal of Black Studies*, among others. Since earning his PhD in 2007, Dr. Palmer has authored/coauthored well over one hundred academic publications. His books include *Racial and ethnic minority students' success in STEM education* (2011, Jossey-Bass), *Black men in college: Implications for HBCUs and beyond* (2012, Routledge), *Black graduate education at HBCUs: Trends, experiences, and outcomes* (2012, Information Age Publishing), *Fostering success of ethnic and racial minorities in STEM: The role of minority serving institution* (2012, Routledge), *Community colleges and STEM: Examining underrepresented racial and ethnic minorities* (2013, Routledge), *STEM models of success: Programs, policies, and practices* (2014, Information Age Press), *Black male collegians: Increasing access, retention, and persistence in higher education* (2014, Jossey-Bass), *Understanding HIV and STI Prevention for College Students* (2014, Routledge), *Black men in higher education: A guide to ensuring success* (2014, Routledge), *Exploring diversity at historically Black colleges and universities: Implications for policy and practice* (2015, Jossey-Bass), *Hispanic serving institutions: Their origins, and present, and future challenges* (2015, Stylus), *The African American students' guide to STEM Career* (forthcoming, Greenwood Publishing), and *Black men in the academy: Stories of resiliency, inspiration, and success* (2015, Palgrave Macmillan). In 2009, the American College Personnel Association's (ACPA) Standing Committee for Men recognized his excellent research on Black men with its Outstanding Research Award. In 2011, Dr. Palmer was named an ACPA Emerging Scholar, and in 2012, he received the Carlos J. Vallejo Award of Emerging Scholarship from the American Education Research Association (AERA). Furthermore in 2012, he was awarded the Association for the Study of Higher Education (ASHE) Mildred García Junior Exemplary Scholarship Award. In 2015, *Diverse Issues in Higher Education* recognized Dr. Palmer as an emerging scholar. Later that year, he also received the SUNY Chancellor's Award for Excellence in Scholarship and Creative Activities. This prestigious award is normally given to a full professor.

Dr. Larry J. Walker is an educational consultant focused on supporting Historically Black Colleges and Universities (HBCUs). Dr. Walker has published scholarly articles, policy, and research briefs. His research examines the impact environmental factors have on the academic performance and social–emotional functioning of students from HBCUs. Dr. Walker's teaching and research background includes working at Howard and Morgan State University. He is a former Congressional Black Caucus Foundation and Congressional Fellow and Legislative Director for former Congressman Major R. Owens. During his tenure on Capitol Hill, Dr. Walker worked on the Education Sciences Reform Act and amendments to the Higher Education Act. In addition, Dr. Walker collaborated with administrators, advocates, policymakers, and researchers to increase funding for HBCUs. He earned his doctorate from Morgan State University.

Dr. Ramon B. Goings is an assistant professor of Educational Leadership at Loyola University, Maryland. His research interests are centered on disrupting deficit narratives about African American students generally and African American males specifically PK–PhD. More specifically, his scholarship explores the following three threads: (1) studying the academic and social trajectory of high-achieving African American males throughout the education pipeline; (2) examining the resiliency of non-traditional students of color in higher education; and (3) exploring the recruitment and retention of African American male K–12 educators and higher education faculty and student affairs practitioners. Dr. Goings's research appears in various outlets, including: *Adult Learning, Diverse: Issues in Higher Education* and the *Journal of African American Males in Education*. Prior to working at UMBC, Dr. Goings was a special education (math and reading) and music teacher and also served as an education policy fellow with the White House Initiative on Educational Excellence for African Americans. In 2015, Dr. Goings was selected as a participant in the Eighth Annual Asa G. Hilliard III and Barbara A. Sizemore Research Institute on African Americans and Education held at the 2015 American Educational Research Association (AERA) annual conference. He is currently the managing editor of the *Journal of African American Males in Education* (JAAME). Dr. Goings earned his doctor of education degree in urban educational leadership from Morgan State

University, master of science degree in human services with a focus in clinical counseling from Post University, and bachelor of arts degree in music education from Lynchburg College.

Charmaine E. Troy is a PhD candidate in higher education at Morgan State University. She was the program coordinator for the Academic Enrichment Program at Morgan State University and a graduate teaching assistant and advisor at North Carolina Central University. Her research focus area is student success, persistence, student development, and the college experience of minorities, particularly black females, at Historically Black Colleges and Universities (HBCUs) and minority-serving institutions (MSIs). She is coauthor of the forthcoming book *Black Female College Students: A Guide to Student Success in Higher Education*. Charmaine earned her MPA in public administration from North Carolina Central University and BA in journalism and mass communication from the University of North Carolina at Chapel Hill.

Chaz T. Gipson received his bachelor of arts degree from Morehouse College with a major in sociology and public health sciences and his master of education degree in educational administration and policy with a minor in curriculum and instruction from Howard University. Mr. Gipson is currently working on his doctoral degree in communications at Howard University with a special focus in higher educational leadership. Currently, Mr. Gipson serves in a dual role as a teaching associate in the Howard University School of Communications and as an education specialist at the US Department of Education in the Office of Post-Secondary Education, where he serves in various capacities to assist low-income individuals, first-generation college students, and persons with disabilities to progress through the academic pipeline from middle school to post-baccalaureate programs. Mr. Gipson's combined interdisciplinary research interest examines educational access and opportunities for African American males and other minority students in K–12 schools and higher education institutions—particularly those attending HBCUs; the role of social media technology in Black student success for both STEM and non-STEM students; investigation of present and post-matriculation of college readiness programs; student leadership development and student affairs practices; African Americans representation in mass media; risky health behaviors of young adults; race, class, and gender issues in media; social justice in educational leadership; and inter/intra-personal communication practices that impacts student success academically, socially, emotionally, and psychologically.

Dr. Felecia Commodore is assistant professor of Educational Foundations and Leadership at Old Dominion University. She earned her PhD in higher education from the University of Pennsylvania's Graduate School of Education. Her research focus area is HBCU leadership, governance, and administrative practices. Dr. Commodore's research interests also lie in leadership in Black communities and the relationship of Black women and leadership. She has a background working as an admissions counselor and academic advisor at Trinity University, Washington, DC, and University of Maryland, College Park, respectively. Currently, Dr. Commodore serves as an independent consultant in the higher education sector. She obtained an MA in higher education administration from the University of Maryland, College Park, Maryland, and a BS in marketing with a minor in sociology from Drexel University in Philadelphia, Pennsylvania. Dr. Commodore is coeditor of *Opportunities and Challenges of Historically Black Colleges and Universities*. She currently has research published in the *Journal of Multicultural Education* and the *Journal of Negro Education*. Dr. Commodore also has written opinion essays for *HBCULifestyle.com, Diverse Issues in Higher Education,* and *The Chronicle of Higher Education*. She is the coeditor of the book *Opportunities and Challenges at Historically Black Colleges and Universities*, recently released by Palgrave Macmillan.

About the Contributors

Dr. Sheree N. Alexander is a K–12 public school administrator and educational researcher and serves as an adjunct faculty member at Rowan University in Glassboro, New Jersey. With twenty-one years of experience in various roles within educational settings, she has served as a language arts literacy teacher, instructional specialist, instructional support officer, and assistant principal in both urban and suburban school districts in Pennsylvania, New Jersey, and Ohio. Dr. Alexander is a recipient of the Gloucester Township Community Service Award and the Martin Luther King Jr. Freedom Medal. Dr. Alexander has been a presenter at the Achievement Gap Midwest Regional Conference in Chicago, Illinois, Roberto Clemente Alternative School in Ann Arbor, Michigan, and provided district-wide professional development for the school district of Philadelphia. Her research interests include building capacity for culturally responsive teaching, critical pedagogy, and creating professional learning communities to improve the schooling experience of students in urban school districts.

Janatus Avonte Barnett is a graduate student at the University of Baltimore, where he is pursuing a master of science degree in negotiations and conflict management. He received his bachelor of science degree from Coppin State University. His scholarly interest is community conflict resolution. His career goal is to become a member of the House of Representatives.

Dr. Tiffany F. Boykin is assistant dean of student services at Anne Arundel Community College and a legal strategist. She has held numerous administrative and teaching assignments on community college and urban research campuses. Prior to higher education, Boykin enjoyed a successful career in broadcast media. Boykin's recent research interests have focused on access, participation, and outcomes for students of color in collegiate settings. Specifically, Boykin has examined graduate education, the role of Historically Black Colleges and Universities, strengths-based teaching models for diverse learners, and legal strategies to maximize urban institutional success. Boykin is a sought-after speaker, has coauthored a book, *Black Graduate Education at Historically Black Colleges and Universities: Trends, Experiences, and Outcomes*, and has published numerous articles; the most recent are entitled: "Examining the Paradox Between Dismantling De Jure Segregation and Affirmative Action: Implications from Contemporary Higher Education Case Law" and "For-profit, For-success, For-Black men: A Review of Literature on Urban For-profit Colleges and Universities." She has received several awards for her contributions to the profession, including recognition by the American Education Research Association for her efforts in producing scholarship that advances multicultural and multiethnic education, and for her continued commitment to underserved communities. Boykin earned a BA in communication from the University of Maryland, College Park, an MS in communications management from Towson University, a PhD in higher education from Morgan State University, and recently, a JD from the University of Baltimore School of Law.

Dr. Julius Davis is an assistant professor of mathematics education in the College of Education at Bowie State University. His research focuses on Black male students' educational experiences and Black male teachers' praxis, educational, and professional experiences.

Kimberly Eldridge is a PhD candidate as well as a special assistant to the president at Trinity University, Washington, DC. Mrs. Eldridge had the pleasure of serving President Obama in the role of special assistant, in the Office of Communications and Outreach, External Affairs at the US Department of Education in Washington, DC. She served in the Obama administration for three and a half years, while also serving as an adjunct professor at the University of the District of Columbia's Community College, where she taught in the Social Sciences Department. After she receives her PhD in educational management with an emphasis on higher education from Hampton University, she plans to continue her higher education journey toward her ultimate goal of becoming a college or university president. Mrs. Eldridge's dissertation topic focuses on HBCUs' sustainable fundraising practices from the development officers' perspective.

Dr. Antonio L. Ellis is an adjunct professor at the College of Charleston School of Education, Health and Human Performance. He holds a BA in religion and philosophy, MA in religious studies, and an MEd in educational leadership and policy Studies. In addition, in May 2013 he earned a doctoral degree in educational leadership and policy studies from Howard University in Washington, DC. His passion is advocating on behalf of students who are speech and language impaired. His research interests are educational leadership and policy, educational foundations, multicultural education, minority higher education institutions, critical race theory in education, and special education.

About the Contributors

Dr. F. Abron Franklin, JD, MPH, currently serves as the director of the Treatment and Prevention Services Division with Volunteers of America Oregon (VOAOR). Dr. Franklin is an epidemiologist with applied experience in injury and forensic epidemiology. He has over ten years of experience in population health and program management in the areas of injury and chronic disease prevention and behavioral health. Dr. Franklin is trained in injury epidemiology and injury prevention from The Johns Hopkins University School of Public Health, Center for Injury Research and Policy, where he received his PhD. He received his MPH in epidemiology and international health from the Morehouse School of Medicine and a BS in biology from Morgan State University. Dr. Franklin has postgraduate training in immunobiology and molecular biology (University of Pennsylvania), immunology (New York University, Cancer Research Center), and epidemiology and the law (The University of Michigan, Ann Arbor) along with postdoctoral training in health leadership and policy (David Satcher Health Leadership Institute, Health Policy Division) and applied forensic epidemiology (Oregon Health & Science University). Dr. Franklin also holds a Juris Doctor from Kline School of Law at Drexel University. Dr. Franklin's research and practice interests include forensic and social epidemiology; public policy and population health; behavioral health; violent crime; abuse-related injuries, and civil rights, race, and law. He has faculty appointments with the Morehouse School of Medicine, Department of Community Health and Preventive Medicine and the Oregon Health and Science University-Portland State University School of Public Health, Epidemiology Division.

Dr. Kimberly Hardy is an assistant professor in the Department of Social Work and Latino Community Practice at the University of Saint Joseph, where she teaches in their newly established MSW program. Dr. Hardy's area of research focuses on religion and spirituality, with a particular emphasis on the historical and contemporary role of the Black church in African American communities. She has conducted trainings, presented workshops, and researched and published in this area for years and is coauthor of a forthcoming book entitled *Toward Shared Goals: Social Work, the Black Church and Collaborations for Effective Practice*. Despite the rich tradition of faith in the foundation of social work practice, this will be only the second book to focus on the intersectionality of faith among African Americans and social work.

Dr. Lamar Hylton serves as the assistant vice provost for student life in the Office for Student Affairs at the University of Minnesota-Twin Cities. In this role, he has oversight of the Office for Fraternity and Sorority Life, the Office for Student Engagement, the Office for Off-Campus Living, as well as commuter student engagement and multicultural student engagement. Dr. Hylton received his bachelor of arts degree in vocal music-performance from Morgan State University in Baltimore, Maryland; a master of education degree in college student personnel from Ohio University in Athens, Ohio; and a doctor of philosophy degree in higher education administration from Morgan State. He has held a variety of administrative roles at Goucher College and the University of North Carolina–Asheville. Dr. Hylton is involved and holds leadership positions, in several civic and professional organizations.

Dr. Stevie L. Lawrence II is a higher education practitioner, researcher, and enthusiast. Dr. Lawrence has served in various capacities in higher education at various types of postsecondary institutions, including community colleges, historically Black institutions, and large comprehensive universities. Currently, he serves as the director of College Success Services with GEAR UP NC at UNC General Administration (System Office) in Chapel Hill, North Carolina. Dr. Lawrence has an affinity for Historically Black Colleges and Universities (HBCUs), as he is a three-time alumnus of these institutions, earning an undergraduate degree in history from North Carolina A&T State University, a master's degree in Public Administration from North Carolina Central University, and a PhD in Urban Higher Education from Jackson State University. His research interests include the effects of mentoring programs on student academic success at both the secondary and postsecondary levels, students' success methods in minority education, college choice among suburban and rural African American high school students, and effective practices for higher education leadership.

Dr. Herbert Robinson Marbury is associate professor of Hebrew Bible and Ancient Israel at Vanderbilt University. His research focuses on biblical interpretation and religion and cultural criticism. Marbury is the author of two books: *Imperial Dominion and Priestly Genius* (Sopher Press, 2012) and *Pillars of Cloud and Fire: The Book of Exodus in African American Biblical Interpretation* (Forthcoming, August, 2015, New York University Press).

Dr. Tara D. Miller completed her PhD at Clark Atlanta University in Humanities and Africana Women's Studies; she earned a master of science degree in English education and a bachelor of science degree in broadcast journalism from Florida A&M University. Her research interests include analyzing 1970s Blaxploitation films, African American history, and the Harlem Renaissance. Dr. Miller has been teaching at the collegiate level for over thirteen years, and she is currently serving in the US Army Reserves as a sergeant, promotable to officer.

Christopher N. Smith is a PhD student in the Department of Sociology and Anthropology at Howard University. The concentrations of his study are social inequalities and criminology. He ultimately seeks to develop research on the manner in which socioeconomic inequalities impact the structure of romantic relationships and families within minority populations.

Index

A&T *see* North Carolina Agricultural and Technical State University
Abernathy, Ralph David 74, 125
accreditation process 85–6
AERA *see* American Educational Research Association
African American Male Achievement Program 107
African Diaspora 128, 129
African Methodist Episcopal 124
Alexander, Michelle 77
Alexander, Sheree 55–69; back home 59–60; Black educators 55–60; challenges of attending an HBCU 65–7; choosing Cheyney University 62–3; cultural responsiveness 60–6; culture 58–9; HBCUs 63–5; predominantly White institutions 57–8 (*see also* predominantly White institutions)
American Educational Research Association (AERA) 43, 82–3, 84, 87, 142
Anderson, Rosa 106
Anthony E. 64
Arbaugh, J. B. 91
Arce, C. H. 30
Arizona State University 49
assistantship 4, 8, 11
attacks 2, 8, 85–6
Aubrey, Harold 73

Bachenheimer, B. 90–1
Bailey, Randall C. 127, 128, 130
Baird, L. L. 28–9
Baldwin, Joseph: "Notes on an Afrocentric Theory of Black Personality" 116–17
Baltimore City Public Schools 39
Barnett, Janatus 39, 51–3

Benedict College 40, 41, 116
Bista, K. 91
Black Algebra I teachers: research 85
Black Atlantic 128, 132n3
Black clergy 125, 126
Black Codes 131n2, 133
Black educators 3, 7, 39, 55–60, 61, 62, 64, 65, 79, 80, 82, 85, 98, 105
Black feminist theory 63
Black Graduate Education at Historically Black Colleges and Universities 1
Black History Month 48
Black intelligentsia 133–40; African Americans and higher education 135–6; Black college aspirations 136–8; HBCU graduate education 138–40; uneducated slave 134–5
Black males counter-narratives 39–54; primary education from Baltimore City Public School, undergraduate and some graduate study at Coppin State University and pursuant of master's degree at University of Baltimore *see* Barnett, Janatus; primary education from Black schools and postsecondary education from HBCUs *see* Ellis, Antonio L.; primary education from PWI and postsecondary education from HBCUs *see* Smith, Christopher N.
Black Panther Party 47
Blackwell, J. E. 30
Black women 63, 144
Bond, Julian 137
Bowie State University 70, 85, 86–7, 88
Bowles, T. A. 102
Boykin, Tiffany F. 25–38; advice for prospective doctoral students 34–6; career objectives 31–4; faculty agency 30–1; "girls like me: 27–8;

motivational factors for school choice 25–8; peer agency 31; pre-entry experiences 29–30; socialization 28–9
Bradley, Ed 74
Bradley, Josephine 116
Braxton, J. 3
Brier, E. M. 3
Brown, D. F. 61
Brown v. Board of Education 55–6, 66, 122, 124, 136, 138
Burke High School 40

Cain, Herman 44
career objectives 31–4; faculty member 33–4; researcher 32–3
Carmichael, Stokley 49, 137
Carr, Gregory 46
Carson, Bill 71–2, 77
Carter, Melanie 48
Case Studies of Urban Algebra I Teachers 85
CAU *see* Clark Atlanta University
Center for Mathematics Education (CfME) 84–5
Cervero, R. M. 102
Cesari, J. P. 31
CfME *see* Center for Mathematics Education
challenges of attending an HBCU 23, 34, 65–7
Charleston County Public Schools 40
Cheyney University 5, 62–3, 65–6, 74, 135
Christianity 48, 105, 127, 129
Christian Methodist Episcopal 124
Chunn, Jay Carrington 73
civil rights 47, 77, 124, 125, 126, 133, 136–8
Civil War 134, 135
Clark Atlanta University (CAU) 115, 117, 120, 123, 125, 130, 131
Coates, Ta-Nehisi 77
Coaxum, J., III 63, 64
cohort-based learning *see* online accelerated cohort program
Common Cause North Carolina 105
Conger, J. A. 63
Congressional Black Caucus Foundation 5
Conrad, C. F. 3
Cooper, Anna Julia 62
Coppin State University 39, 51–3, 70
costs, educational 16–17, 52, 97, 99, 100, 103
Cox, D. 91

critical race theory 63, 83, 84, 146
criticism of HBCUs 2, 8, 85–6
cultural responsiveness 60–6
culture 52, 58–9, 121, 129; Black 48; Black man 3; dominant 41, 63; family 98; fluency-dominated 46; graduate 11, 28, 30, 51, 58; hegemonic 60; institution 17, 18, 23, 28, 61, 106; religion 131; undergraduate 102
Cunningham, M. C. J. 59

Davis, Angela 49
Davis, Julius 79–89; advice for graduate students 87–8; attack on HBCUs 85–6; Black faculty and graduate students support of research 82; Black male research 86–7; dissertation 84; doctoral student publication 83–4; family influence to attend HBCU 79–80; HBCUs contribution to diversification in workforce 86; interaction with senior Black scholars at colloquium 83; mentorship 80–1; oppression of Black middle school students 84; post-doctoral experience with research 84–5; scholarly development at AERA conference 83; studying issues of race and racism at Morgan 81–2; tenure 85; writing for AERA annual conference 82–3
desegregation 56, 63, 66
Different World, A 70–1
Dillard, C. B. 47
diversification in workforce 85, 86
doctorate degrees: at a school of theology *see* Marbury, Herbert Robinson; in the Southeast *see* Eldridge, Kimberly R.; statistics 21, 32; undergraduate degree and doctoral at the same institution *see* Hylton, Lamar; undergraduate degree at a PWI and doctoral at HBCU *see* Alexander, Sheree; *see also* Black males counter-narratives
Dore, T. M. 29
Dred Scott v. Sanford 134, 135
Du Bois, W. E. B. 46, 49, 52, 139; *Souls of Black Folks* 122
Dunson, Carrie 98

Economic Opportunity Act 102
Edelman, Marion Write 137
Eggleston, Laura 134
Eldridge, Kimberly R. 90–100

Ellis, Antonio L. 39, 40–8; Black male and speech impaired at a PWI 41–2; epistemological foundation as a Black male 45–8; HBCUs for graduate education 42–3; Howard University to Georgetown University 40–2; K–12 40; misleading assumptions about HBCUs 44–5; recommendations 48; social justice-driven graduate education 43–4; success stories of HBCU 45
Emory University 125; Candler School of Theology 131
England, R. 61
epistemological foundation 63; Black male 45–8
Ethridge, S. B. 56
Euro-American students 57
Evans, W. Franklin 108
Evers, Medgar 137
E. W. Rhodes school 60
Exodus 127–8, 131n2

faculty agency 30–1
faculty members AERA conference 83; Black 82, 85; difficult 19, 27; ethnicity 4; feedback 20, 28–9, 93; mentorship 11, 18, 19, 85, 87, 111; racism 81, 82; White 82, 116
faculty-student interactions 2, 30
family 70, 71, 79, 88, 100, 114, 124, 125, 129; environment 4, 61, 72, 91, 95, 98, 111; expectations 48, 58, 59; influence 79–80; -like 31; no 34; support 4, 6
FAMU *see* Florida Agricultural and Mechanical University
Felder, Cain Hope 46
Florida Agricultural and Mechanical University (FAMU) 70, 113–14, 115, 116, 117, 123; Feeder Program 115
Florida State University 114
Flowers, A. 106
Fountaine, T. P. 2, 103; *Black Graduate Education at Historically Black Colleges and Universities* 1
Franklin, Robert 120–1
Frazier, E. Franklin 137
Frederick, Wayne A. I. 45
Freire, P. 62
Fuller, J. 90–1

Gammon Theological Seminary 124, 125
Garibaldi, A. M. 64
Garrison, D. R. 91

Garvey, Marcus 46
Gendrin, D. 105
Georgetown University 10, 45; School of Liberal Arts 41, 42–3
Gilroy, Paul 132n3
Gipson, Chaz T.: "How Do Health Beliefs Affect health Behaviors among African American Male College Students" 10; personal scholarly narrative 9–11
Gipson, Regina 11
"girls like me" 27–8
Goings, Ramon: personal scholarly narrative 6–8
Golde, C. M. 29
Goldhaber, D. 64
Graduate Student Association (GSA) 74
Grambling State University 70, 110
grants; US Department of Education 43; writing 51, 85, 86
Graves, Earl G. 74
Gray, Freddie 6, 79, 84, 86
Griffin, Ervin V., Sr. 108
GSA *see* Graduate Student Association

Hamer, Fannie Lou 46, 125
Hamilton, C. V. 81
Hampton University 70, 93–9, 107, 108
Hardy, Kimberly 70–78; academic program 73–6; advice and recommendations 77–8; career preparation 76–7; destiny at Morgan State University 72–3; different world 70–2; positive experiences 74–5
Harkless, John 44
Hart, M. 90–1
Hayti Heritage Center 105
Hicks, Terence vii–viii
Higher Education Act 45, 102
Hilton, A. A.: *Black Graduate Education at Historically Black Colleges and Universities* 1
Holland, Spencer 71
Houston, Charles Hamilton 137–8
Howard, Oliver O. 117
Howard University 5–6, 43, 44, 45, 48, 49, 50–1, 70, 103, 115, 117, 122, 137; Legal Department 137; School of Divinity 40–1; sit-in 50, 57
Hughes, Langston 137
Humphries, Frederick S. 114, 121
Hurston, Zora Neale 137
Hylton, Lamar 15–24; advice for prospective doctoral students 23–4; believe in yourself 22; critical

thinking skills 21; Morgan State University 15–24; convenience 16; cost 16–17; familiarity 16–18; seize the moment 22–3; self-doubt 18–20; university pride 20–1

inner-city youth 59
intelligentsia, Black *see* Black intelligentsia
Interdenominational Theological Center (ITC) 124–31
Irvine, J. J. 56–7

Jackson, Jessie, 44
Jackson, Maynard 121
Jackson State University (JSU) 107, 108, 109–10, 111, 112
Jencks, C. 117
Jim Crow 131n2, 133, 137
Johnson-Bailey, J. 102
John-Wesley, Howard 46
Jones, Absalom 131n2
Jones, Felicia 114
Jones, Lois-Harrison 48
Jones, W. A. 66
Jordan, Barbara 74
JSU *see* Jackson State University

Kanungo, R. A. 63
Kearsley, G. 93
King, Colbert L. 44
King, Martin Luther, Jr. 46, 120, 121, 125, 128, 137
King. S. H. 55, 57, 64
Knight-Pulliam, Keisha 122

Ladson-Billings, Gloria 44, 87
Lawrence Steve L., II 102–12; deciding to earn PhD 107–11; "Factors That Influence Alumni Giving at Two Historically Black Universities in North Carolina" 111; making graduate school selection 103; making transition as graduate student 103–6; NCCU preparing students for the future 106–7; support in dissertation phase 111; undergraduate and preparing for graduate school 102–3
leadership 29, 43, 48, 53, 62–3, 64, 65, 74, 75, 92, 93, 94, 109, 136–7, 138–9; religious 125, 126, 131
Lee, Spike 44, 74
Lincoln University 80

literature review 2–11
Lowder, L. 90–1
Lynn, Lonnie Rashid, Jr. 44

Manning, W. H. 30
Marbury, Herbert Robinson: theological education at a Black graduate school 124–32
Marshall, Thurgood 65, 122, 137, 138
Martin, Elmer 72, 77
Mays, Benjamin E. 113, 120, 121
McCloud, Linard 46
McNair, Cheryl 10
McNair, Ronald 10; *see also* Ronald E. McNair Award of Excellence; Ronald E. McNair Post-Baccalaureate Scholarship Program; Ronald McNair Scholar
McPhatter, Anna 72, 73
Meier, K. 61
Miller, James 114
Miller, Lillie 114
Miller, Kelly 49
Miller, Tara D. 113–23; academic journey and critics 116–17; awkward academic experience 115–16; critical and stellar graduates of HBCUs 122; doctoral studies 115; false accusations 113–15; list of HBCUs 118–19; professors' advice and influence of Robert Franklin 120–1; realization about Howard University 117; recommendations 122; reflection journey not traveled 117
Millersville University 55
misleading assumptions about HBCUs 44–5
Moore, Brian D. 46
Moore, M. 93
Morehouse College 44, 70, 117, 120–2, 125, 137; School of Medicine 136; School of Religion 124; Upward Bound Math and Science Southeastern Regional Institute 102
Morgan State University 5, 6–7, 8, 9, 15–24, 27, 28, 29, 31–6, 44, 70–81, 84, 87, 88, 107, 136; race and racism 81–2; School of Education and Urban Studies 80
Morris Brown College 117, 125
Morrison, Toni 44, 74, 126; "A Humanist View" 131n1
Murray v. Pearson 138

Index

National Board for Professional Teaching Standards 64
National Science Foundation 85
NC A&T *see* North Carolina Agricultural and Technical State University
Neihbuhr, Reinhold 46
Nelms, C. 104
Newton, Huey P. 49
Noguera, P. 59
North Carolina Agricultural and Technical State University (NC A&T) 102–3, 105, 106, 107, 108, 109, 122
North Carolina Central University 9, 103
nurturing relationships 5, 18, 19, 26, 28, 43, 46, 52, 60, 62, 91, 98, 105, 112, 113, 117, 121, 139

Old National United Methodist Church 129, 130
online accelerated cohort program 90–101; academic and internship phase 92–3; advice and recommendation 99–100; author's perception of best practices of Hampton University PhD program 97–8; career preparedness 94; committee selection 92; comparing PWIs and HBCUs 98–9; comprehensive exams 93; dissertation phase 93–4; educational management program students' perspectives 94–7; motivation to purse graduate degree at HBCU 90; online and cohort experience 90–1; residency experience 91–2

Palmer, Robert T. 2, 43, 106; *Black Graduate Education at Historically Black Colleges and Universities* 1; personal scholarly narrative 3–5
Patrick Henry Middle School 59–60
Patterson, G. 104
peer agency 31
Perkins, Claude G. 108
Perry, D. 68
Plessy, Homer 135
Plessy v. Ferguson 135, 136
postsecondary degrees 64
predominantly white institutions (PWIs) 1, 2, 3, 4, 5, 7, 8, 12, 13, 15, 17, 26, 27, 34, 39, 43, 48, 49, 50, 52, 53, 57–8, 62, 64, 65, 66, 67, 85, 90, 98, 108, 113, 116, 123, 125, 138; Black male and speech impaired PWI 41–2
pre-entry experiences 27, 29–30
Public Alley 105

racism 45, 56, 59, 64, 74, 79, 81–2, 83–4, 126, 137
Reconstruction 124, 131n2
residence life 11, 15, 16
Rice, Jerry 44
Riesman, D. 117
Riley, J. 34, 106
Riley, Joseph P. 40
Risner, M. 90–1
Ronald E. McNair Award of Excellence 10
Ronald E. McNair Post-Baccalaureate Scholarship Program 10
Ronald McNair Scholar 11
Rucker, M. 105

Scheurich, J. 47
school choice 25–8
science, technology, engineering, and mathematics (STEM) professionals 86, 103
Scott, Dred 134–5
Scott, J. 106
self-doubt 9, 18–20, 22
Shabazz, Abdulalim Abdullah 80
Siddle-Walker, V. 61
slavery 3, 78, 113, 127, 128, 131n2, 133, 134–5
Smith, Christopher N. 39, 48–51; difficulties of HBCU graduate schools 50–1
socialization 28–9, 30
social justice 5, 6, 43–4, 46, 49, 62, 63, 54, 77, 137
Southeastern Association of Educational Opportunity Program (SAEOPP) 10
speech impediment 40; PWI 41–2, 46
Spelman College 44, 70, 117, 122, 125, 137
Spencer, M. B. 59
STEM professionals *see* science, technology, engineering, and mathematics (STEM) professionals
Stewart, J. 61
student loans 16–17
Suggs, Mr. 72, 77
Swanson, D. P. 59

154 Index

Talley, Dr. 72, 77
tenure 5, 29, 56, 72, 79, 83, 85, 88, 105, 113, 114, 121, 136
theological education at a Black graduate school 124–32
Thompson, John W. 74
Tirmazi, Taqi 75
T'Ofori-Atta, Ndugu G. B. 128
TRIO-Talent Search 10, 11
Troy, Charmaine: personal scholarly narrative 8–9
Ture, K. 81
Twinning, Mary 115

underrepresented 10, 27
United Methodist 124, 125; *see also* Old National United Methodist Church
University of Baltimore 39, 52
University of Pennsylvania 107
Upward Bound 10, 102
U.S. Supreme Court 56, 124; *see also Brown vs. Board of Education of Topeka*

Valentine, T. 102
value of HBCUs 113–23; academic journey and critics 116–17; awkward academic experience 115–16; critical and stellar graduates of HBCUs 122; doctoral studies 115; false accusations 113–15; list of HBCUs 118–19; professors' advice and influence of Robert Franklin 120–1; realization about Howard University 117; recommendations 122; reflection journey not traveled 117
Vanderbilt University 130, 131
Virginia Union University 108

Walker, Alice 74
Walker, Larry J. 7; personal scholarly narrative 5–6
Warner, Neari 110, 111
West, C. 133; "The Dilemma of the Black Intellectual" 47
West African Christianity 129
West Baltimore 79, 81, 84
Whelchel, L. Henry 130
Whiteness 40, 41, 42, 45, 46, 47, 48, 49, 53
Williams, Howard 114
Williams, Juan 74; *Eyes on the Prize* 137
Williams, Willie T. 114
Winfrey, Oprah 122
Winthrop, Jordan 122

Young, Andrew 125
Young, M. 47